INTERNATIONAL VOCABULARY OF MUSIC

LEXIQUE MUSICAL INTERNATIONAL
INTERNATIONAL VOCABULARY OF MUSIC
LESSICO MUSICALE INTERNAZIONALE
INTERNATIONALES MUSIKLEXIKON
VOCABULARIO MUSICAL INTERNATIONAL

Par, by, da, von, por :

Stephen DEMBSKI
Gérard GUBISCH
Jorge LABROUVE
Patrick MARCLAND
Diogène RIVAS

BARNES & NOBLE BOOKS
A DIVISION OF HARPER & ROW, PUBLISHERS
New York, Cambridge, Philadelphia, San Francisco
London, Mexico City, São Paulo, Sydney

A previous edition of this book was published in Paris by Editions Transatlantiques in 1979. It is here reprinted by arrangement.

First BARNES & NOBLE BOOKS edition published 1984.

Library of Congress Cataloging in Publication Data

Lexique musical international.
  International vocabulary of music.

  (Everyday handbook)
  Reprint. Originally published: Paris : Editions transatlantiques, 1979.
  In English, French, German, Italian, and Spanish.
  1. Music—Dictionaries—Polyglot.   2. Dictionaries, Polyglot.   I. Dembski, Stephen.
II. Title.   III. Series.
ML108.L49   1984   780'.3   83-47593
ISBN 0-06-463585-6 (pbk.)

84 85 86 87 88   10 9 8 7 6 5 4 3 2 1

FRANÇAIS

INDEX ALPHABETIQUE

Se reporter au chapitre
TRADUCTIONS
à l'aide du numéro
placé devant chaque terme.

FRANÇAIS

A

N°	
243	Bloc de bois
333	Bois de l'archet
335	Boite à violon
182	Bombarde
240	Bongo
439	Boucle
89	Bouche fermée
713	Bourdon
838	Bourrée
499	Branle
411	Bras de lecture
721	Broderie
440	Bruit blanc
442	Bruit de fond
441	Bruit rose
300	Buffet (orgue)
183	Bugle

C

737	Cadence
740	Cadence imparfaite
739	Cadence parfaite
741	Cadence plagale
742	Cadence rompue
738	Cadentiel
230	Caisse claire
232	Caisse claire avec timbre

N°	
231	Caisse claire sans timbre
233	Caisse roulante
985	Calques
856	Canon
860	Cantate
928	Caractère
251	Castagnettes
877	Cassation
404	Cassette
843	Cavatine
207	Célesta
959	Césure
841	Chaconne
154	Chalumeau
427	Chambre d'écho
645	Changement de mesure
103 872	Chanson
104	Chanson folklorique
48	Chant
323	Chanterelle
67	Chanteur
65	Chanteuse
91	Chant-parlé
66	Chantre
124	Chef d'attaque
76	Chef de chant
73	Chef de choeur
123	Chef de pupitre
118	Chef d'orchestre

N°	
772	Contrepoint renversable
763	Contrepoint simple
766	Contrepoint triple
769	Contrepoint première espèce
767	Contrepoint quadruple
777 790	Contre-sujet
654	Contretemps
172	Contre-tuba
990	Copie musicale
991	Copiste
136	Cor anglais
159	Cor d'harmonie
322	Corde
157	Cor de basset
311	Cordes frottées
346	Cordes pincées
324	Cordier
150 151	Cornemuse
164	Cornet
165	Cornettiste
160	Corniste
496	Corps de ballet
987	Correcteur
941	Coulé
192	Coulisse
329	Coup d'archet
94	Coup de langue
854	Couplet

N°	
832	Courante
250	Crécelle
92	Cri
332	Crin de l'archet
1001	Critique Musical
605	Croche
727	Croisement
149	Cromorne
208	Crotale
209	Crotales
158	Cuivres
795	Culmination
730	Cycle des quintes ascendantes
731	Cycle de quintes descendantes
252	Cymbale
244	Cymbalum
249	Cymbale Charleston
246	Cymbale chinoise
245	Cymbales choquées
248	Cymbale turque
247	Cymbales suspendues

D

N°	
490	Danse
494	Danseur/se
371	Déchant
504	Déchiffrer

E

F

N°	
822	Forme lied
809	Forme Musicale
254	Fouet
37	Fréquence
784	Fugue
785	Fugué

G

839	Gaillarde
342	Gambiste
516 700	Gamme
682	Gamme par tons
681	Gamme pentatonique
835	Gavotte
396	Générateur de sons
845	Gigue
221	Glockenspiel
255	Gong
293	Grand jeu
775	Grand mélange
929	Grave
51	Grave (voix)
993	Graveur
450	Graves
436	Gravure (disque)
992	Gravure musicale
105	Grégorien
256	Grelots
234	Grosse caisse

N°	
131	Groupe des bois
310	Groupe des cordes
158	Groupe des cuivres
115	Groupe des vents
668	Grupetto
979	Guidon
241	Guimbarde
350	Guitare
395	Guitare basse
394	Guitare électrique
351	Guitariste

H

153	Harmonica
155	Harmonica à bouche
695	Harmonie
17	Harmoniques
696	Harmonisation
281	Harmonium
347	Harpe
348	Harpiste
414	Haut-parleur
135	Hautbois
137	Hautbois d'amour
138	Hautboïste
63	Haute-contre
186	Hélicon
36	Hétérophonie

N°		N°	
893	Laude	327	Manche
410	Lecture	362	Mandoline
935	Léger	257	Maracas
931	Lent	898	Marche
660	Levée de temps	723	Marche harmonique
629	Ligature		
628	Ligatures	220	Marimba
508	Ligne	215	Marimbaphone
510	Ligne supplémentaire	337	Martelé
627 962	Liaison	978	Matériel d'orchestre
761	Libre	588	Médiante
940	Lié	359	Médiator
101	Litanie	774	Mélange
451	Longueur d'onde	102	Mélisme
946	Louré	686	Mélodie
360	Luth	2	Mélomane
999	Luthier	834	Menuet
675	Lydien	214	Métallophone
365	Lyre	486	Metteur en scène
		634	Métrique
		635	Métronome
		862	Messe
		637	Mesure

M

N°		N°	
868	Madrigal	640	Mesure binaire
430	Magnétophone	639	Mesure composée
268	Mailloche	638	Mesure simple
498	Maître de ballet	641	Mesure ternaire
75	Maître de chant	57	Mezzo-soprano
74	Maître de chapelle	519	Mi
580	Majeur	538	Mi bémol
		426	Microcontact

N°	
565	Micro-intervalle
424	Microphone
406	Microsillon
530	Mi dièse
554	Mi double bémol
546	Mi double dièse
581	Mineur
423	Mixage
676	Mixolydien
294	Mixtures
672	Mode
933	Modéré
680	Modes ecclésiastiques
743	Modulation
97	Monodie
415	Monophonie
422	Montage
669	Mordant
861	Motet
905	Motif
653	Mouvement
807	Mouvement contraire
806	Mouvement parallèle
50	Moyenne (voix)
434	Multi-pistes
418	Multiphonie
90	Murmure
836	Musette
1	Musicien
969	Musicologie

N°	
970	Musicologue
4 367	Musique ancienne
5 374	Musique baroque
378	Musique de chambre
6	Musique classique
9	Musique concrète
8 375	Musique contemporaine
483	Musique de scène
12	Musique de variété
3	Musique instrumentale
7	Musique romantique
803	Mutation

N

370	Neumes
577	Neuvième
452	Niveau
884	Nocturne
453	Nœud
604	Noire
916	Non mesuré
594	Notation
597 908	Notation carrée
907	Notation proportionnelle
758	Note ajoutée

N°	
865	Passion
610	Pause
194	Pavillon
277 758	Pédale
298	Pédalier
146 190	Perce
198	Percussionniste
197	Percussions
456	Période
932	Pesant
132	Petite flûte
670	Petites notes
961	Phrasé
808	Phrase Musicale
677	Phrygien
271	Pianiste
270	Piano
273	Piano à queue
272	Piano droit
401	Piano électrique
288	Pieds. (8, 16, etc.)
947	Piqué
432	Piste
193	Piston
407	Plage (sur disque)
100	Plain chant
358	Plectre
938	Plus vite
984	Pochette
849	Poème symphonique

N°	
624	Point
649	Point d'arrêt
648	Point d'orgue
96	Polyphonie
88	Port de voix
507	Portée
720	Position
899	Pot-pourri
331	Poussé
954	Précis
827	Prélude
982	Première fois
314	Premiers violons
717 794	Préparation
421	Prise de son
913	Procédé de liquidation
725	Progression ascendante
726	Progression descendante
457	Propagation du son
912	Prosodie
364	Psaltérion
866	Psaume
122	Pupitre

Q

493	Quadrille
417	Quadriphonie
608	Quadruple-croche
614	Quart de soupir

N°	
566	Quart de ton
571	Quarte
619	Quartolet
384 885	Quatuor
385	Quatuor à cordes
573	Quinte
732	Quintes cachées
386	Quintette
387	Quintette à vent
620	Quintolet

R

N°	
728	Rapport avec la sous-dominante mineure
994	Rastral
518	Ré
537	Ré bémol
470	Récital
79	Récitant
80 867	Récitatif
910	Récurrence
529	Ré dièse
553	Ré double bémol
545	Ré double-dièse
981	Réduction
793	Réexposition
853	Refrain
485	Régisseur

N°	
287	Registration
24 83 108	Registre
909	Renversement
911	Renversement récurrent
968	Renvoi
473	Répétiteur
472	Répétition
783 802	Réplique
963	Reprise
796	Réponse
863	Requiem
718	Résolution
458	Résonance
459	Résonateur
87 958	Respiration
719	Retard
429	Réverbération
988	Révision
887	Rhapsodie
762	Rigoureux
852	Ritournelle
886	Romance
602	Ronde
824	Rondeau
844	Rondo
352	Rosace
968	Roulade
213	Roulement (de timbale)
630	Rythme

S

		N°	
30	S'accorder	377	Série
475	Salle de concert	188	Serpent
924	Sans lenteur	927	Serré
923	Sans presser	621	Sextolet
917	Sans rigueur	388	Sextuor
833	Sarabande	523	Si
187	Sarrusophone	542	Si bémol
460	Saturation	534	Si dièse
894	Sautereau	558	Si double bémol
338	Sautillé	550	Si double-dièse
180	Sax-Horn	840	Sicilienne
174	Saxophone	93	Sifflement
176	Saxophone alto	260	Sifflet
178	Saxophone baryton	600	Signes musicaux
179	Saxophone basse	609	Silence
175	Saxophone soprano	355	Sillet
177	Saxophone ténor	405	Sillon
181	Saxophoniste	461	Sinusoïdale (onde)
693	Scander	258	Sirène
694	Scansion	574	Sixte
482	Scène	733	Sixte napolitaine
888	Scherzo	521	Sol
259	Scie musicale	540	Sol bémol
569	Seconde	532	Sol dièse
315	Seconds violons	556	Sol double-bémol
616	Seizième de soupir	548	Sol double dièse
575	Septième	121	Soliste
622	Septolet	502 596	Solfège
389	Septuor	503	Solfier
744	Séquence	38	Solmisation
592	Sensible	821	Sonate
889	Sérénade		

ALPHABETICAL INDEX

AMERICAN / ENGLISH

Consult chapter
TRANSLATIONS
with the number
indicated before each term.

AMERICAN / ENGLISH

A

C

N°		N°	
727	Crossing (of voices)	444	Density
715	Cross relation	371	Descant
208	Crotale	344	Descant viol
209	Crotales	726	Descending progression
604	Crotchet	942	Detached
92	Cry	797	Development
528	C sharp	537	D flat
195	Cuivre	564	Diatonic
795	Culmination	684	Diatonicism
642	Cut time	584	Diminished
436	Cutting (records)	708	Diminished-seventh chord
730	Cycle of fifths, ascending	939	Diminuendo
731	Cycle of fifths, descending	781	Diminution
810	Cyclical form	120	Direct
810	Cyclic form	486	Director
252	Cymbal	445	Discontinuous
244	Cymbalum	736	Dissonance
		112 949	Divided
		798 823	Divertimento
		112	Divisi
		553	D double flat
		517	Do
		376	Dodecaphonic music

D

N°		N°	
518	D	590	Dominant
490	Dance	673	Dorian
494	Dancer	624	Dot
948	Dampen	625	Dotted note
278	Damper	837	Double
545	D double sharp	647	Double bar
585	Degree	320	Double bass
607	Demisemiquaver	321	Double bass player

N°	
715	False relation
80	Falsetto
879	Fantasy
714	Fauxbourdon
514	F clef
555	F double flat
547	F double sharp
648	Fermata
471	Festival
539	F flat
595	Figuration
752	Figured bass
859	Figured choral tune
755	Figures/Figuring
152	Fife
573	Fifth
448	Filter
855	Finale
327 353	Fingerboard
276 356	Fingering
123	First chair
123	First desk
982	First time
314	First violins
156	Flageolet
535	Flat
134	Flautist
771	Florid counterpoint
133	Flute
295	Flute stop

N°	
134	Flutist
104	Folk-song
288	Foot/Feet (8-foot stop - 16 foot stop, etc...)
43	Force
759	Foreign note
449	Formant
299	Foundation stops
571	Fourth
761	Free
768	Free counterpoint
917	Freely
37	Frequency
829	French ouverture
334	Frog
531	F sharp
784	Fugue
785	Fugue-like
293	Full organ
746	Fundamental

G

N°	
521	G
839	Galliard
835	Gavotte
512	G clef
556	G double flat
548	G double sharp
308	German zither
540	G flat

N°		N°	
845	Gigue	348	Harpist
753	Given bass	279	Harpsichord
210	Glockenspiel	280	Harpsichordist
221		932	Heavy
255	Gong	334	Heel
670	Grace notes	487	Helden tenor
273	Grand piano	186	Helicon
929	Grave	608	Hemidemisemiquaver
105	Gregorian	36	Heterophony
405	Groove	710	Hexachord
756	Ground bass	732	Hidden fifths
532	G sharp	323	Highest string
979	Guide score	249	High cymbal
350	Guitar	438	Highs
351	Guitarist	273	High tam-tam
		63	High tenor
		49	High (voices)
		648	Hold
		921	Holding back

H

		146	Hole
603	Half note	190	
720	Half-position	95	Homophony
611	Half rest	160	Horn player
337	Hammered	871	Hymn
263	Hard drumstick	674	Hypodorian
153	Harmonica		
155			
723	Harmonic movement		
17	Harmonics		

I

696	Harmonization	782	Imitation
281	Harmonium	740	Imperfect cadence
695	Harmony	477	Impresario
347	Harp	882	Impromtu
364		902	Improvisation

N°		N°	
936	Lively	638	Measure in
227	Log drum	588	Mediant
439	Loop	102	Melisma
414	Loudspeaker	222	Membranophone
946	Loure	214	Metallophone
450	Lows	634	Metric
238	Low tam-tam	694	Metrical scansion
51	Low (voice)	912	Metrical structure
874	Lullaby	635	Metronome
360	Lute	636	Metronome mark
999	Luthier	57	Mezzo-soprano
675	Lydian	519	Mi
365	Lyre	406	Microgroove
		565	Microinterval
		424	Microphone
		50	Middle (voice)
		603	Minim

M

N°		N°	
868	Madrigal	581	Minor
431	Magnetic tape	834	Minuet
580	Major	70	Mixed choir
63	Male alto	423	Mixing
362	Mandolin	676	Mixolydian
53	Man's voice	774	Mixture
257	Maracas	294	Mixture stop
898	March	672	Mode
220	Marimba	933	Moderate
215	Marimbaphone	734	Modulation
962	Mark	415	Mono
862	Mass	97	Monody
978	Material	415	Monophonic
637	Measure	422	Montage/splicing
655	Measured	669	Mordent

N°	
938	More lively
875	Morning music
861	Motet
905 967	Motif
905	Motive
89	Mouth closed
155	Mouth organ
144 189	Mouthpiece
653	Movement
925	Moving
418	Multiphonic
434	Multi-track
90	Murmur
836	Musette
990	Music copying
991	Music copyist
483	Music for the theatre
2	Music lover
506	Music theory
1001	Musical critic
505	Musical dictation
992	Musical engraving
809	Musical form
808	Musical phrase
973	Musical publication
259	Musical saw
600	Musical signs
1	Musician
970	Musicologist
969	Musicology

N°	
9	Musique concrete
803	Mutation
294	Mutation stop
147 191 336	Mute

N

559	Natural
733	Neapolitan sixth
412	Needle
410	Needle and cartridge
370	Neumes
709	Neutral chord
577	Ninth
884	Nocturne
453	Node
721	Nonharmonic tones
904	Notate
594	Notation
515	Notes
599	Note-shapes
916	Not measured
355	Nut
334	Nut of the bow

O

392	Obbligato
135	Oboe
137	Oboe d'amore

P

N°	
291	Pedal coupler
354	Peg (tuning)
681	Pentatonic scale
197 199	Percussion
198	Percussionist
739	Perfect cadence
20	Perfect pitch
456	Period
961	Phrased
677	Phrygian
271	Pianist
270	Piano
132	Piccolo
359	Pick
441	Pink noise
201	Pitched instruments
741	Plagal cadence
100	Plain chant
204	Plate bells
468	Player
358	Plectrum
346	Plucked string instruments
976	Pocket score
96	Polyphony
88	Portamento
946	Portato
899	Potpourri
720	Position
285	Positive organ
954	Precise
827	Prelude

N°	
717 794	Preparation
123	Principal
986	Proof
987	Proofreader
457	Propagation of sound
907	Proportional notation
866	Psalm
364	Psaltery

Q

493	Quadrille
417	Quadraphonic
767	Quadruple counterpoint
619	Quadruplet
604	Quarter note
612	Quarter rest
566	Quarter tone
384 885	Quartet
492	Quartet (ballet)
605	Quaver
386	Quintet
620	Quintuplet
918	Quickening

R

919	Rallentando
15 16 965	Range
21	Range of voice
250	Rattle

N°		N°	
518	Re	963	Reprise
470	Recital	863	Requiem
867	Recitatif	718	Resolution
79	Recitation	458	Resonance
99	Recitative	459	Resonator
867	Recitativo	796	Response
403	Record	609	Rest
148	Recorder	32	Retune
419 436	Recording	31	Retuned
		429	Reverberation
421	Recording by microphone	988	Revision
409	Record player	887	Rhapsody
910	Recurrence	630	Rhythm
911	Recurrence inversion	967	Rhythmic fragment
981	Reduction	689	Rhythmic group
145	Reed	631	Rhythmic value
296	Reed stop	762	Rigorous
793	Re-exposition	852	Ritornello
853	Refrain	213	Roll (of the kettle drum)
24 83 108	Register	886	Romance
		7	Romantic music
		824	Rondeau
287	Registration	824 844	Rondo
472	Rehearsal		
473	Rehearsal coach	968	Roulade
728	Relation of the sub-dominant minor		
703	Relative key		
19	Relative pitch		**S**
703	Relative tonality		
802 964	Repeat	338	Saltando
		894	Saltarello
783	Replica	833	Sarabande

N°		N°	
247	Suspended cymbals	27	Tempered
719	Suspension	633	Tempo
903	Sustain	653	
926	Sustained	59	Tenor
849	Symphonic poem	233	Tenor drum
847	Symphony	177	Tenor saxophone
114	Symphony orchestra	167	Tenor trombone
773	Syncopated counterpoint	578	Tenth
632	Syncopation	644	Ternary division
464	Synchronization	641	Ternary meter
402	Synthesizer	16	Tessitura
690	System	593	Tetrachord
		812	Thematic, Thematicism
		813	
		811	Theme
		570	Third
		567	Third tone
		607	Thirty-second note
		615	Thirty-second rest
		523	Ti (si)
		627	Tie (Overmetric division)
		927	Tighten
		42	Timbre
		211	Timpani
		212	Timpanist
		235	Tom-tom

T

N°		N°	
324	Tailpiece	745	Tonal functions
225	Tambourin	699	Tonality
224	Tambourine	561	Tone
229		411	Tone arm
236	Tam-tam	94	Tonguing
430	Tape recorder	586	Tonic
75	Teacher	775	Total mixture
25	Temperament		

N°	
341	Viola da gamba
342	Viola da gamba player
343	Viola d'amore
312	Violin
335	Violin case
313	Violinist
317	Violist
897	Virelai
469	Virtuoso
47	Vocal art
75	Vocal coach
86	Vocalize
47	Vocal technique
46	Voice
711	Voice-leading
303	Voix celeste
303	Vox angelica

N°	
487	Wagnerian tenor
895	Waltz
454	Wave
451	Wave-length
659	Weak beat
254	Whip

N°	
93 260	Whistle
440	White noise
602	Whole note
610	Whole rest
561	Whole step
682	Whole-tone scale
387	Wind quintet
115	Wind section
383	Wind trio
923	Without hurrying
917	Without rigor
924	Without slowness
52	Woman's voice
243	Wood-block
264	Wooden drumstick
333	Wood of the bow
131	Woodwind section

218	Xylophone
219	Xylophonist

Z

364	Zither

ITALIANO

INDICE ALFABETICA

Consultare il capitolo
TRADUZIONE
reperandosi al numero indicato.

ITALIANO

A

608	Biscroma
814	Bitematico
243	Blocco di legno
89	Bocca chiusa
144	Bocchino
189	
182	Bombarda
186	Bombardone
240	Bongo
721	Bordatura
713	Bordone
196	Bouché
838	Bourrée
411	Braccio
499	Brando
602	Breve

C

737	Cadenza
740	Cadenza imperfetta
739	Cadenza perfetta
742	Cadenza rotta
741	Cadenza sospesa
738	Cadenzato
645	Cambio de misura
427	Camera d'eco
206	Campanaccio
202	Campane
204	Campane di placche
256	Campanella

210	Campanelli
221	
203	Campane tubolari
856	Canone
65	Cantante
860	Cantata
368	Cantilena
48	Canto
105	Canto gregoriano
91	Canto parlato
100	Canto pieno
66	Cantore
67	
103	Canzone
853	
872	
104	Canzone folclorica
355	Capotasto
928	Carattere
300	Cassa
414	Cassa acustica
232	Cassa colla corda
230	Cassa chiara
239	
233	Cassa rulante
231	Cassa senza corda
404	Cassette
251	Castagnette
843	Cavatina
354	Caviglia
207	Celesta
154	Cennamella
959	Cesura

N°		N°	
365 366	Cetra	900	Composizione
		468	Concertista
249	Charleston	467 846	Concerto
511 701	Chiave		
		980	Conduttore
996	Chiave d'accordare	800	Conseguente
513	Chiave di do	501	Conservatorio
514	Chiave di fa	735	Consonanza
512	Chiave di sol	443	Continuo
512	Chiave di violino	321	Contrabassista
350	Chitarra	320	Contrabasso
395	Chitarra bassa	892	Contradanza
394	Chitarra elettrica	792	Contraesposizione
351	Chitarrista	143	Contrafagotto˙
691	Chironomia	488	Contrafigura
196	Chiusi	58 63	Contralto
841	Ciaccona		
730	Ciclo di quinte ascententi	760	Contrappunto
731	Ciclo di quinte descendenti	764	Contrappunto composto
755	Cifrato	765	Contrappunto doppio
309	Cister a tastiera	771	Contrappunto fiorito
363	Cistre tiorbato	768	Contrappunto libero
139	Clarinetto	769	Contrappunto prima specie
140	Clarinettista	767	Contrappunto quadruplo
279	Clavicembalo	772	Contrappunto rovesciabile
280	Clavicembalista	763	Contrappunto semplice
805	Coda	773	Contrappunto sincopato
952	Colore	766	Contrappunto triplo
329	Colpo d'arco	654	Contratempo
94	Colpo di lingua	172	Contratuba
380	Complesso strumentale	777 778 790	Contrassoggetto
26	Comma		
901	Compositore		

N°	
990	Copia musicale
991	Copista
69 857	Corale
858	Corale con variante
859	Corale florido
322	Corda
324	Cordiera
497	Coreografo
72	Corista
150	Cornamusa
164 184	Cornetta
165	Cornettista
160	Cornista
159	Corno
157	Corno di bassetto
136	Corno inglese
68	Coro
70	Coro misto
648	Corona
649	Corona sull'silenzio
496	Corpo di ballo
832 884	Corrente
987	Correttore
192	Coulisse
332	Crini dell'arco
1001	Critica musicale
606	Croma
563	Cromatico
683	Cromatismo
149	Cromorno

N°	
209	Crotali
208	Crotalo
417	Cuadrofonia
195	Cuivré
795	Culminazione

D

490	Danza
494	Danzatrice
494	Danzatore
504	Decifrare
578	Decima
444	Densita
801	Desinenza
85	Detonare
505	Dettato musicale
21	Diapason
564	Diatonico
684	Diatonismo
527	Diesis
584	Diminuito
781	Diminuzione
45	Dinamica
118	Direttore d'orchestra
119	Direzione d'orchestra
120	Dirigere
989	Diritto d'autore
62 371	Discanto
403	Disco

N°	
445	Discontinuo
736	Dissonanza
276	Diteggiatura
356	
798	Divertimento
823	
112	Divisi
517	Do
536	Do bemolle
376	Dodecafonismo
528	Do diesis
552	Do doppio bemolle
544	Do doppio diesis
590	Dominante
734	Dominante secondarie
786	Doppia fuga
647	Doppia sbarra
339	Doppie corde
837	Doppio
551	Doppio bemolle
71	Doppio coro
543	Doppio diesis
626	Doppio punto
673	Dorico
41	Durata
617	Duina
381	Duo

E

N°	
428	Eco
973	Edizione musicale

N°	
437	Elettroacustica
446	Emissione del suono
702	Enarmonia
678	Eolico
966	Episodio
500	Equilibrio
710	Esaccordo
791	Esposizione
950	Espressione
22	Estensione
185	Eufonio
54	Evirato

F

N°	
520	Fa
1000	Fabbricante di archi
998	Fabbricante di strumenti
997	Fabbricazione di strumenti
539	Fa bemolle
531	Fa diesis
555	Fa doppio bemolle
547	Fa doppio diesis
142	Fagottista
141	Fagotto
715	Falsa relazione
80	Falsetto
685	Falso
714	Falso bordone
116	Fanfara

G

H

281	Harmonium
186	Helicon
36	Heterofonia
95	Homofonia

I

144 189	Imboccatura
782	Imitazione
882	Impromptu
903	Improvvisatore
902	Improvvisazione
724	Incatenamento
689 967	Inciso
993	Incisore
436 992	Incisione
727	Incrosciamento
636	Indicazione metronomica
420	Ingegnere di suono
447	Ingresso
869 871	Inno
679	Ionico
674	Ipodorico
953	In rilievo
880	Interludio
881	Intermezzo
560	Intervallo

N°

43	Intensità
28 30	Intonare
27	Intonato
25 84	Intonazione
850	Introduzione
883	Invenzione

L

522	La
541	La bemolle
533	La diesis
557	La doppio bemolle
549	La doppio diesis
930	Largo
893	Laude
940 941	Legato
627 628 629 962	Legatura
935	Leggiero
122	Leggio
333	Legno
931	Lento
410	Lettura
660	Levare
761 917	Libero
675	Lidio

N°	
508	Linea
510	Linea addizionale
145	Lingua
221	
361	Lira
365	
101	Litania
999	Liutaio
360	Liuto
452	Livello
985	Lucidi
451	Lunghezza d'onda

M

868	Madrigale
473	Maestro concertatore
498	Maestro di ballo
75	Maestro di canto
74	Maestro di capella
73	Maestro di coro
580	Maggiore
362	Mandolino
327	Manico
257	Maracas
898	Marcia
220	Marimba
337	Martellatto
978	Materiale di orchestra
268	Mazzuolo
50	Media

N°	
588	Mediante
102	Melisma
686	Melodia
2	Melomane
774	Mescolanza
862	Messa
214	Metallofono
634	Metrica
694	
635	Metronomo
57	Mezzo-soprano
519	Mi
538	Mi bemolle
426	Microcontatto
424	Microfono
565	Microintervallo
406	Microsolco
530	Mi diesis
554	Mi doppio bemolle
546	Mi doppio diesis
604	Minima
581	Minore
834	Minuetto
423	Miscela
676	Missolidio
639	Misura
640	Misura binaria
643	
641	Misura ternaria
644	
672	Modo
933	Mederato
680	Modi ecclesiastici

N°		N°	
743	Modulazione	970	Musicologo
418	Multifonia	836	Musetta
937	Molto vivace	803	Mutazione
97	Monodia		
415	Monofonia		

N

422	Montaggio		
669	Mordente	251	Nacchere
90	Mormorio	431	Nastro magnetico
905	Motivo	370	Neumi
861	Mottetto	874	Ninnananna
653	Movimento	453	Nodo
723	Movimento armonico	577	Nona
807	Movimento contrario	758	Nota aggiunta
711	Movimento di voci	625	Nota puntata
806	Movimento parallelo	598	Nota quadrata
434	Multipiste	904	Notare
		759	Nota strana
4 367	Musica antica	515	Note
		594	Notazione
5 374	Musica barocca	907	Notazione proporzionale
6	Musica classica	597 908	Notazione quadrata
9	Musica concreta	884	Notturni
8 375	Musica contemporanea	952	Nuance
378	Musica da camera		

O

877	Musica di caccia		
483	Musica di scena	392	Obbligato
12	Musica popolare	135	Oboe
7	Musica romantica	137	Oboe d'amore
3	Musica strumentale	138	Oboista
1	Musicista	454	Onda
969	Musicologia		

P

N°	
619	Quartina
566	Quarto di tono
573	Quinta
732	Quinte nascoste
386	Quintetto
387	Quintetto per fiati
620	Quintina
250	Raganella
919	Rallentando
728	Rapporto colla sottodo minante minore
887	Rapsodia
994	Rastral
518	Re
537	Re bemolle
470	Recitale
79	Recitante
99 867	Recitativo
529	Re diesis
553	Re doppio bemolle
545	Re doppio diesis
485 486	Regista
430	Registratore
287 419	Registrazione
292	Registri dell'organo
24 83 108	Registro
783 802	Repplica

R

N°	
863	Requiem
87 958	Respirazione
988	Revisione
910	Ricusa
981	Riduzione
793	Riesposizione
762	Rogoroso
963	Ripetizione
718	Risoluzione
458	Risonanza
459	Risonatore
796	Risposta
920	Ritardando
719	Ritardo
921	Ritenuto
630	Ritmo
852 853 897	Ritornello
429	Riverberazione
909	Rivoltato
886	Romanza
824 844	Rondo
352	Rosa
911	Rovesciamento ricorrenre
914	Rubato
213	Rullo
440	Rumore bianco
442	Rumore di fondo
441	Rumore rose

S

475	Sala		

N°		N°	
475	Sala	259	Sega
866	Salmodia	600	Segni musicali
894	Saltarello	964	Segno
338	Saltellatto	603	Semibreve
364	Salterio	607	Semicroma
833	Sarabanda	605	Semiminima
187	Sarrusofono	720	Semiposizione
181	Sassofonista	562	Semitone
174	Sassofono	592	Sensibile
178	Sassofono baritono	923	Senza affretare
179	Sassofono basso	916	Senza mesura
176	Sassofono contralto	924	Senza rallentare
175	Sassofono soprano	917	Senza rigore
177	Sassofono tenore	949	Separato
460	Saturazzione	744	Sequenza
180	Sax Horn	889	Serenata
646	Sbarra	377	Serie
241	Scacciapensieri	188	Serpentone
516 700	Scala	574	Sesta
		733	Sesta napoletana
681	Scala pentatonica	388	Sestetto
682	Scala per toni	621	Sestina
693	Scandire	575	Settima
335	Scatola di violino	622	Settimina
482	Scena	389	Settimino
888	Scherzo	523	Si
32	Scordare	542	Si bemolle
31	Scordato	840	Siciliana
594	Scrittura	534	Si diesis
569	Seconda	558	Si doppio bemolle
983	Seconda volta	550	Si doppio diesis
315	Secondi violini	218	Silofono

N°	
215	Silorimba
632	Sincopa
464	Sincronizzazione
847	Sinfonia
848	Sinfonia da camera
402	Sintetizzatore
258	Sirena
253	Sirena di fischietto
690	Sistema
357	Smanicare
948	Smorzare
301	Soffieria
463	Soffio
789	Soggetto
521	Sol
540	Sol bemolle
405	Solco
532	Sol diesis
556	Sol doppio bemolle
548	Sol doppio diesis
503	Solfeggiare
502 596	Solfeggio
121	Solista
38	Solmisazione
256	Sonaglio
821	Sonate
40	Sonorita
591	Soppraddominante
344	Soppra la viola
62 56	Soprano
587	Sopratonica

N°	
147 191 278 336	Sordina
926	Sostenuto
589	Sottodominante
435	Sovra impressione
509	Spazio
267	Spazzolini
282	Spinetta
331	Spinto
942	Staccato
416	Stereofonia
804	Stretto
851 854	Strofa
127	Strumentazione
115	Strumenti a fiato
201	Strumenti a percussione determinata
242	Strumenti a percussione indeterminata
222	Strumenti di pelle
393	Strumenti elettronici
107	Strumentista
106	Strumento
878	Studio
825	Suite
399	Suonatore di onde Martenot
162	Suonatore di tromba
342	Suonatore di viola da gamba
13	Suono
196	Suono chinso
195	Suono metallico

N°		N°	
440	Suono bianco	656	Tempo libero
797	Sviluppo	59	Tenore
		487	Tenore wagneriano
		506	Teoria della musica
		570	Terza

T

		618	Terzina
		567	Terzo di tono
334	Tallone dell'arco	16	Tessitura
225	Tamburello	593	Tetracordo
229	Tamburello a sonagli	221	Timbre
224	Tamburino	42	Timbro
223	Tamburo	211	Timpani
224	Tamburo basco	212	Timpanista
227	Tamburo di legno	192	Tiro
228	Tamburo frottato	276	Tocco
226	Tamburo militare	235	Tom-tom
236	Tam-tam	699	Tonalità
237	Tam-tam acuto	586	Tonica
238	Tam-tam grave	561	Tono
269 275	Tastiera	703	Tono relativo
		330	Trascinare
353	Tasto	971	Trascrizione
274 349	Tavola d'armonia	111	Trasportare
		109	Traspositore
789 811	Tema	110	Trasposizione
		261	Triangolo
815	Tema con variazioni	297	Tribuna dell'organo
813	Tematico	373	Tricinium
812	Tematismo	671	Trillo
633	Tempo	382	Trio
655	Tempo controllato	383	Trio di ance
659	Tempo debole	787	Triplo fuga
658	Tempo forte		

N°		N°	
572	Tritono	216	Vibrafono
161	Tromba	943	Vibrare
163	Tromba bassa	466	Vibrazione
162	Trombetista	896	Villanella
166	Trombone	316	Viola
168	Trombone contralto	341	Viola da gamba
169	Trombone basso	343	Viola d'amore
167	Trombone tenore	313	Violinista
170	Tromboniste	312	Violino
171	Tuba	317	Violista
302	Tubi	319	Violoncellista
173	Tubista	345	
		318	Violoncello

U

		897	Virelai
579	Undecima	960	Virgola
820	Unione	469	Virtuoso
568	Unisono	936	Vivace
462	Uscità	86	Vocalizzo
		46	Voce

V

		55	Voce bianca
		303	Voce celeste
34	Valore acustico	54	Voce di castrato
631	Valore ritmico	52	Voce femenina
601	Valori di durata	55	Voce infantile
895	Valzer	53	Voce maschile
816	Variazione	81	Voce parlata
817	Variazione continua	712	Voci intermediarie
818	Variazione ornamentale	125	Volta di pagina
819	Variazione per amplificazione		
465	Ventre		
217	Vibrafonista		

W

243	Wood Block

X

Z

DEUTSCH

LPHABETISCHES SACHREGISTER

Die vor jedem
Fachausdruck erwähnte
Nummer verweist auf Kapitel
ÜBERSETZUNGEN..

DEUTSCH

A

N°		N°	
148	Blockflöte	536	C es
328	Bogen	552	C eses
333	Bogenholz	841	Chaconne
1000	Bogenmacher	928	Charakter
329	Bogenstrich	249	Charleston becken
240	Bongo	691	Cheioromie
838	Bourrée	246	Chinesisches becken
316	Bratsche	68	Chor
317	Bratschist	69	Choral
930	Breit	857	
922	Breiter werdend	73	Chordirektor
598	Brevis	73	Chordirigent
721	Broderie	497	Choreograph
182	Brummbass	72	Chorsänger
241	Brummeisen	683	Chromatik
480	Buffo-oper	563	Chromatisch
483	Bühnenmusik	528	C is
		544	C isis
		366	Cister
C		754	Continuo
		892	Contratanz
517	C	493	Contretanz
856	Canon	832	Corrente
66	Cantor	832	Courante
896	Canzonetta		
251	Castagnettes		
843	Cavatine	**D**	
207	Celesta		
303		518	D
319	Cellist	344	Damengeige
318	Cello	948	Dämpfen
280	Cembalist	147	Dämpfer
279	Cembalo	191	
		336	

H

N°	
140	Klarinesttist
6	Klassische musik
269	Klaviatur
270	Klavier
470	Klavierabend
995	Klavier-stimmschlüssel
239	Kleine militärtrommel
209	Kleine tanzbecken
231	Kleine trommel ohne schnarrsaite
232	Kleine trommel mit schnarrsaite
230	Kleine trommel
820	Kleine oberleitung
371	Kniegeige
805	Koda
479	Komische oper
26 960	Komma
901	Komponist
900	Komposition
9	Konkrete musik
501	Konservatorium
735	Konsonanz
426	Kontaktmikrophon
320	Kontrabass
321	Kontrabassist
172	Kontrabasstuba
143	Kontrafagott
760	Kontrapunkt
769	Kontrapunkt der ersten gattung
773	Kontrapunkt mit synkopierter gegenstimme

N°	
777	Kontrasubjekt
467 846	Konzert
273	Konzertflügel
468	Konzertgeber
468	Konzertist
124	Konzertmeister
475	Konzertraum
475	Konzertsaal
476 477 489	Konzertverwalter
991	Kopist
987	Korrektur
986	Korrekturbogen
910	Krebs
911	Krebsumkehrung
527	Kreuz
727	Kreuzung
149	Krummhorn
206	Kuhglocken
192	Kulisse
338	Kurz gestossen und betont
979	Kustos

L

N°	
720	Lage
931	Langsam
919	Langsamer werdend
406	Langspielplatte

N°		N°	
968	Läufer	362	Mandola
360	Laute	52	Männerstimme
414	Lautsprecher	289	Manual koppler
43	Lautstärke	257	Maracas
413	Lautverstärker	898	Marsch
935	Leicht	220	Marimba
659	Leichter takkteil	215	Marimbaphon
365	Leier	933	Mässig bewegt
230	Leinen trommel	241	Maultrommel
592	Leitton	588	Mediante
343	Liebesgeige	814	Mehrfacher tematik
822	Liedartig	418	Mehrkanalig
103 872	Liedchen	434	Mehrspürig
		96	Mehrstimmigkeit
470	Liederabend	770 788	Mehrstimmig
629	Ligatur		
628	Ligaturen	102	Melisma
508	Linie	682	Melodie
913	Liquidierungsprozess	907	Mensural notation
101	Litanei	834	Menuett
893	Lobgesänge	862	Messe
146 190	Löcher	214	Metallophon
		634	Metrik
917	Löcker	635	Metronom
675	Lydisch	636	Metronomzahl
		424	Mikrophon
		226	Militärtrommel
		720	Mittellage

M

868	Madrigal	712	Mittel stimmen
410	Magnettonabtaster	50	Mittlerestimme
431	Magnettonband	676	Mixolydisch
430	Magnettongerät	774	Mixtur

N

8 375	Moderne Musik
743	Modulation
672	Modus
581	Moll
97	Monodie
422	Montage
669	Mordant
875	Morgenständchen
861	Motette
905	Motiv
153 155	Mundharmonika
144 189	Mundstück
90	Murmeln
836	Musette
990 991	Musikabschreiben
600	Musikalischen zeichen
259	Musikalische säge
881	Musikalisches zwischenspiel
1	Musiker
505	Musikdiktat
1001	Musikkritiker
2	Musikliebhaber
970	Musikschrifsteller
506	Musiktheorie
973	Musikverlag
969	Musikwissenschaft
803	Mutation

N°

782	Nachahmung
800	Nachfolgende stimme
429	Nachhall
733	Neapolitanische sext
734	Nebendominanten
966	Nebenmotiv
294	Nebenstimme
526	Nebenvorzeichnung
507	Netenlinien
370	Neumen
709	Neutraler akkord
923	Nicht beschleunigen
924	Nicht schleppen
884	Nokturne
577	None
515 596	Noten
601	Notendauer
599	Noten figuren
507	Notenleiter
993	Notenstecher
992	Notenstich
601	Notenwert
507	Notenzeile
594	Notierung
952	Nuance

O

17	Obertöne
587	Obertonika
392	Obligat

N°	
961	Phrasierung
677	Phrygisch
271	Pianist
132	Piccolo flöte
947	Pikiert
741	Plagalschluss
204	Platteglocken
408	Plattenteller
358 359	Plektrum
96	Polyphonie
166	Posaune
170	Posaunist
899	Potpourri
954	Präzis
827	Präludium
299	Prinzipal
472	Probe
912	Prosodie
866	Psalm
364	Psalter
122	Pult
182	Pummer
624	Punkt
625	Punktierte note

Q

417	Quadraphon
597 908	Quadratnotation
598	Quadrat note
492	Quadratschritt tanzschritt

N°	
493	Quadrille
571	Quart
750	Quartenschritt
384 885	Quartett
619	Quartole
707	Quartsextakkord
133	Querflöte
152	Querpfeife
715	Querstand
753	Quint
323	Quinte
751	Quintenschritt
731	Quintenzirkel abwärts
730	Quintenzirkel aufwärts
386	Quintett
620	Quintole

R

936	Rasch
994	Rastral
416	Raumklang
463	Rausch
989	Rechte
981	Reduzierung
485 486	Regisseur
24 83 108	Register
436	Register kanzelle
287	Registratur

ESPAÑOL

INDICE ALFABETICO

Remitirse al capitulo
TRADUCCIONES
ayudado por el numero
ubicado delante de cada término.

ESPAÑOL

A

N°	
760	Contrapunto
764	Contrapunto compuesto
767	Contrapunto cuádruple
769	Contrapunto de primera especie
765	Contrapunto doble
771	Contrapunto florido
768	Contrapunto libre
763	Contrapunto simple
773	Contrapunto sincopado
772	Contrapunto reversible
775	Contrapunto total
766	Contrapunto triple
777 778 790	Contrasujeto
654	Contratiempo
172	Contratuba
990	Copia musical
991	Copista
69 857	Coral
859	Coral florido
858	Coral variado
605	Corchea
623	Corchete
324	Cordal
497	Coreógrafo
72	Corista
151	Cornamusa
164 184	Corneta
165	Cornetista

N°	
160	Cornista
159	Corno
157	Corno di bassetto
136	Corno inglés
68 297	Coro
70	Coro mixto
986	Corrección
987	Corrector
832	Corrente
832	Courante (Fr.)
332	Crin del arco
1001	Crítica musical
563	Cromático
683	Cromatismo
149	Cromorno
208	Crotalo
209	Crotalos
727	Cruzamiento
598	Cuadrada
417	Cuadrafonia
571	Cuarta
384 885	Cuarteto
385	Cuarteto de cuerdas
566	Cuarto de tono
619	Cuatrillo
322	Cuerda
311	Cuerdas frotadas
346	Cuerdas pellizcadas
346	Cuerdas punteadas
496	Cuerpo de baile
795	Culminación

634 694	Métrica
635	Metrónomo
423 774	Mezcla
57	Mezzo-soprano
519	Mi
538	Mi bemol
565	Microintervalo
424	Micrófono
425	Micrófono bidireccional
426	Micrófono de contacto
406	Microsurco
554	Mi doble bemol
546	Mi doble sostenido
834	Minué
862	Misa
863	Misa de difuntos
530	Mi sostenido
676	Mixolidio
933	Moderado
672	Modo
680	Modos eclesiasticos
743	Modulación
97	Monodia
415	Monofonía
422	Montaje
669	Mordente
861	Motete
905	Motivo
925	Moviendo
653	Movimiento

807	Movimiento contrario
806	Movimiento paralelo
418	Multifonía
434	Multipista
90	Murmullo
836	Musette (Fr.)
4 367	Música antigua
5 374	Música barroca
6	Música clásica
9	Música concreta
8 375	Música contemporánea
378	Música de cámara
483	Música de escena
3	Música instrumental
12	Música ligera
7	Música romántica
1	Músico
969	Musicología
970	Musicólogo
803	Mutación
937	Muy vivo

N

604	Negra
370	Neumas
452	Nivel
884	Nocturno
758	Nota agregada

Q

573	Quinta
732	Quintas superpuestas
386	Quinteto
387	Quinteto de vientos
620	Quintillo
691	Quironomía

R

919	Ralentando
887	Rapsodia
994	Rastral (Regla de copista con pentagrama incluído)
518	Re
537	Re bemol
470	Recital
79	Recitante
99 867	Recitativo
910	Recurrencia
239	Redoblante
213	Redoble
553	Re doble bemol
369	Redobles
545	Re doble sostenido
602	Redonda
981	Reducción
793	Reexposición
287	Registración
24 83 108	Registro
292	Registros (organo)

728	Relación con la subdominante menor
963	Repeticón
435	Replay
783 802	Réplica
863	Requiem
718	Resolución
459	Resonador
458	Resonancia
529	Re sostenido
87 958 960	Respiración
796	Respuesta
920	Retardando
719	Retardo
429	Reverberación
988	Revisión
762	Riguroso
897	Ringellied (Al.)
921	Ritenuto
630	Ritmo
852	Ritornello
886	Romance
824	Rondeau
844	Rondo
352	Roseta
440	Ruido blanco
442 463	Ruido de fondo
441	Ruido rosa
213 439	Rulo

S

T

LEXIQUE MUSICAL INTERNATIONAL

INTERNATIONAL VOCABULARY OF MUSIC

LESSICO MUSICALE INTERNAZIONALE

INTERNATIONALES MUSIKLEXIKON

VOCABULARIO MUSICAL INTERNATIONAL

TRADUCTIONS
TRANSLATIONS
TRADUZIONE
ÜBERSETZUNGEN
TRADUCCIONES

N°	FRANCAIS	AMERICAN ENGLISH	ITALIANO	DEUTSCH	ESPAÑOL
1	MUSICIEN	MUSICIAN	MUSICISTA	MUSIKER	MÚSICO
2	Mélomane	Music lover	Melomane	Musikliebhaber	Melómano
3	MUSIQUE INS-TRUMENTALE	INSTRUMEN-TAL MUSIC	MUSICA STRU-MENTALE	INSTRUMENTAL MUSIK	MÚSICA INS-TRUMENTAL
4	Musique ancienne	Early Music	Musica antica	Altere Musik	Música antigua
5	Musique Baroque	Baroque Music	Musica Barocca	Barok Musik	Música Barroca
6	Musique classique	Classical Music	Musica Classica	Klassische Musik	Música clásica
7	Musique Romantique	Romantic Music	Musica romantica	Romantische Musik	Música romántica
8	Musique contemporaine	Contemporary music	Musica contemporanea	Moderne Musik	Música contemporánea
9	Musique concrète	Musique concrète	Musica concreta	Konkrete Musik	Música concreta
10	Aléatoire	Aleatoric	Aleatoria	Aleatorisch/Vom Zufall Abhängig	Aleatoria(o)
11	Atonale	Atonal	Atonale	Atonal	Atonal
12	Musique de variété	Light music	Musica popolare	Schlagermusik	Música ligera
13	SON	SOUND	SUONO	KLANG	SONIDO
14	Source sonore	Sound source	Fonte sonora	Klangquelle	Medio sonoro
15	Ambitus	Ambitus Range	Ambito	Bereich Umfang	Ambito
16	Tessiture	Tessitura Range	Tessitura	Höhenlage	Tesitura
17	Harmoniques	Harmonics Overtones	Armonici	Obertöne	Armónicos
18	Oreille	Ear	Orecchia(o)	Ohr Gehör	Oído Oreja
19	Oreille relative	Relative pitch	Orecchio relativo	Relatives gehör	Oído relativo
20	Oreille absolue	Absolute pitch Perfect pitch	Orecchio assoluto	Absolutes gehör	Oído absoluto
21	Diapason	Octave Range of voice Concert pitch Tuning fork	Diapason	Stimmgabel	Diapasón
22	Etendue	Limits of range	Estensione	Umfang	Extensión
23	Amplitude	Amplitude	Amplitudine	Weite Amplitude	Amplitud
24	Registre	Register	Registro	Register	Registro

N°	FRANCAIS	AMERICAN ENGLISH	ITALIANO	DEUTSCH	ESPAÑOL
25	Tempérament	Temperament	Intonazione	Temperierung	Afinación
26	Comma	Comma	Comma	Komma	Coma
27	Tempéré	Tempered	Intonato	Temperiert	Afinado Temperado
28	Accorder	To tune	Intonare	Stimmen	Afinar
29	Accordé	Tuned, in tune	Accordato	Gestimmt	Afinado
30	S'accorder	To tune	Intonare	Zusammen stimmen	Afinar
31	Désaccordé	Retuned out of tune	Scordato	Verstimmt	Desafinado
32	Désaccorder	To retune	Scordare	Verstimmen	Desafinar
33	Acoustique	Acoustic	Acustica	Akustik Akustisch	Acústica
34	Valeur acoustique	Acoustical value	Valore acustico	Akustischer wert	Valor acústico
35	Assonance	Assonance	Assonanza	Assonanz Gleichklang	Asonancia Asonanza
36	Hétérophonie	Heterophony	Heterofonía	Heterophonie	Heterofonía
37	Fréquence	Frequency	Frequenza	Frequenz	Frecuencia
38	Solmisation	Solmization	Solmisazione	Solmisation	Solmisación
39	Attaque	Attack	Attacco	Anschlag	Ataque
40	Sonorité	Sonority	Sonorità	Klangfülle	Sonoridad
41	Durée	Duration	Durata	Dauer	Duración
42	Timbre	Timbre	Timbro	Klangfarbe	Timbre
43	Intensité	Intensity Force	Intensità	Stärke Lautstärke	Intensidad
44	Toucher	Touch (Keyboard)	Forma d'attacco	Tasten	Forma de ataque
45	Dynamique	Dynamic	Dinamica	Dynamik	Dinámica
46	VOIX	VOICE	VOCE	STIMME	VOZ
47	Art vocal	Vocal art Vocal technique	Arte vocale	Gesangskunst	Arte vocal Técnica vocal
48	CHANT	SINGING SONG	CANTO	GESANG	CANTO
49	Aiguë (voix)	High (voice)	Voce acuta	Hohe stimme	Voz aguda
50	Moyenne (voix)	Middle (voice)	Voce media	Mittlerestimme	Voz media
51	Grave (voix)	Low (voice)	Voce grave	Tiefe stimme	Voz grave
52	Voix de femme	Woman's voice	Voce feminina	Frauenstimme	Voz femenina
53	Voix d'homme	Man's voice	Voce maschile	Männerstimme	Voz de hombre

N°	FRANCAIS	AMERICAN ENGLISH	ITALIANO	DEUTSCH	ESPAÑOL
54	Voix de castrat	Castrato voice	Voce di castrato Evirato	Kastratstimme	Voz de castrado
55	Voix d'enfant	Children's voice	Voce infantile Voce bianca	Kinderstimme	Voz de niño
56	Soprano	Soprano	Soprano	Sopran	Soprano
57	Mezzo-soprano	Mezzo-soprano	Mezzo-soprano	Tiefer Sopran	Mezzo-soprano
58	Contralto	Contralto	Contralto	Altstimme	Contralto
59	Tenor	Tenor	Tenore	Tenor	Tenor
60	Baryton	Baritone	Baritono	Bariton	Barítono
61	Basse	Bass	Basso	Bass	Bajo
62	Dessus	Treble	Discanto Soprano (Inst.)	Diskant Diskantstimme	Tiple
63	Haute-contre	High tenor Male alto Countertenor	Contralto	Altsänger	Contraalto
64	Basse-contre	Contrabass	Basso profondo	Tiefer bass	Bajo profundo
65	Chanteuse	Singer (female)	Cantante	Sängerin	Cantante
66	Chantre	Cantor	Cantore	Cantor Vorsänger	Cantor
67	Chanteur	Singer (male)	Cantore	Sänger	Cantante
68	CHOEUR	CHOIR	CORO	CHOR	CORO
69	Chorale	Chorale	Corale	Choral	Coral
70	Choeur mixte	Mixed choir	Coro misto	Gemischter chor	Coro mixto
71	Double choeur	Double choir	Doppio coro	Doppelchor	Doble coro
72	Choriste	Chorus member	Corista	Chorsänger	Corista
73	Chef de choeur	Choral conductor	Maestro di coro	Chordirigent Chordirektor	Director de coro
74	Maître de chapelle	"Kappelmeister" Conductor	Maestro di capella	Kapellmeister	Maestro de capilla
75	Maître de chant	Vocal coach Teacher	Maestro di canto	Gesanglehrer	Maestro de canto
76	Chef de chant	Choral director	Guida di corda	Gesangleiter Gesangeinstudierung	Guía de cuerda
77	Accompagnement	Accompaniment	Accompagnamento	Begleitung	Acompañamiento
78	Accompagnateur	Accompanist	Accompagnatore	Begleiter	Acompañante
79	Récitant	Recitation-Singer	Recitante	Sprecher	Recitante

N°	FRANCAIS	AMERICAN ENGLISH	ITALIANO	DEUTSCH	ESPAÑOL
80	Voix de fausset	Falsetto	Falsetto	Falsetstimme	Falsete
81	Voix parlée	Spoken voice	Voce parlata	Sprechstimme	Voz hablada
82	Articulation	Articulation	Articolazione	Gliederung	Articulación
83	Registre	Register	Registro	Register	Registro
84	Intonation	Intonation	Intonazione	Intonierung	Entonación
85	Détoner	To sing off pitch Out of tune	Detonare	Detonieren	Desentonar
86	Vocalise	Vocalize	Vocalizzo	Vokalisiren Stimmübung	Vocalización
87	Respiration	Breath	Respirazione	Atmung	Respiración
88	Port de voix	Portamento	Portamento	Hinüberziehen der stimme	Portamento
89	Bouche fermée	Mouth closed	Bocca chiusa	Geschlossener Mund	Boca "chiusa"
90	Murmure	Murmur	Mormorio	Murmeln Gemurmel	Murmullo
91	Chant-parlé	Speech song	Canto parlato	Sprechgesang	Canto hablado
92	Cri	Cry Shriek Shout	Grido	Schrei	Grito
93	Sifflement	Whistle	Fischio	Pfeifen	Silbido
94	Coup de langue	Tonguing	Colpo di lingua	Zungenschlag	Golpe de lengua
95	Homophonie	Homophony	Homofonia	Homophonie	Homofonía
96	Polyphonie	Polyphony	Polifonia	Polyphonie Mehrstimmigkeit	Polifonía
97	Monodie	Monody	Monodia	Monodia	Monodia
98	Antiphonie	Antiphony	Antifonia	Antiphonie	Antifonía
99	Récitatif	Recitative	Recitativo	Rezitativ	Recitativo
100	Plain chant	Plain chant	Canto piano	Gregorianischer Choral	Canto llano
101	Litanie	Litany	Litania	Litanei	Letanía
102	Mélisme	Melisma	Melisma	Melisma	Melisma
103	Chanson	Song	Canzone	Liedchen	Canción
104	Chanson folklorique	Folk-song	Canzone folclorica	Volkslied	Canción folklórica
105	Grégorien	Gregorian	Canto gregoriano	Gregorianik	Canto gregoriano
106	INSTRUMENT	INSTRUMENT	STRUMENTO	INSTRUMENT	INSTRUMENTO
107	Instrumentiste	Instrumentalist	Strumentista	Instrumentist	Instrumentista

N°	FRANCAIS	AMERICAN ENGLISH	ITALIANO	DEUTSCH	ESPAÑOL
108	Registre	Register	Registro	Register	Registro
109	Transpositeur (instrument)	Transposing instrument	Traspositore	Transponierende Instrumente	Instrumento transpositor
110	Transposition	Transposition	Trasposizione	Transposition	Transposición
111	Transposer	To transpose	Trasportare	Transponieren Umsetzen	Transportar
112	Divisé	Divided Divisi	Divisi	Geteilt	Dividido
113	ORCHESTRE	ORCHESTRA	ORCHESTRA	ORCHESTER	ORQUESTA
114	Orchestre symphonique	Symphony orchestra	Orchestra sinfonica	Symphonisches Orchester	Orquesta sinfónica
115	GROUPE DES VENTS	WIND SECTION	STRUMENTI A FIATO	BLASINSTRU-MENTE	INSTRUMENTOS DE VIENTO
116	Fanfare	Brass Band	Fanfara	Fanfare	Fanfarria
117	Orchestre d'harmonie	Concert Band	Orchestra d'armonia	Blasorchester	Orquesta de armonía
118	CHEF D'ORCHESTRE	CONDUCTOR	DIRETTORE D'ORCHESTRA	DIRIGENT KAPELLMEISTER	DIRECTOR DE ORQUESTA
119	Direction d'orchestre	Orchestral conducting	Direzione d'orchestra	Orchesterleitung Dirigieren	Dirección de orquesta
120	Diriger	Conduct Direct	Dirigere	Dirigieren	Dirigir
121	SOLISTE	SOLOIST	SOLISTA	SOLIST	SOLISTA
122	Pupitre	Stand	Leggio	Pult	Atríl
123	Chef de pupitre	Principal First desk First chair	Guida di leggio	Erster solist	Guía de cuerda
124	Chef d'attaque	Concert-master	Guida di corda	Konzertmeister	Guía de ataque
125	Tourne (de page)	Page-turn	Volta di pagina	Seiteumwenden	Vuelta de página
126	Tourneur de page	Page-turner	Asistente di pagina	Seiteumwender	Asistente de pagina
127	INSTRUMEN-TATION	INSTRUMEN-TATION	STRUMENTA-ZIONE	INSTRUMENTAL-KUNDE INSTRUMENTIER-UNG	INSTRUMEN-TACÍON
128	ORCHESTRA-TION	ORCHESTRA-TION	ORCHESTRA-ZIONE	ORCHESTRATION ORCHESTRIEREN	ORQUESTA-CÍON

N°	FRANCAIS	AMERICAN ENGLISH	ITALIANO	DEUTSCH	ESPAÑOL
129	Orchestrateur	Orchestrator	Orchestratore	Orchestrer Instrumentieren Orchestrieren	Orquestador Instrumentador
130	Arrangeur	Arranger	Arrangiatore	Bearbeiter	Arreglador Arreglista
131	GROUPE DES BOIS	WOODWIND SECTION	GRUPPO DEI LEGNI	HOLZINSTRU-MENTE	GRUPO DE MADERAS
132	Petite flûte	Piccolo	Flauto piccolo Ottavino	Piccolo flöte	Piccolo Flautín
133	Flûte	Flute	Flauto	Flöte Querflöte	Flauta
134	Flûtiste	Flutist Flautist	Flautista	Flötist	Flautista
135	Hautbois	Oboe	Oboe	Oboe	Oboe
136	Cor anglais	English Horn	Corno Inglese	Englischhorn	Corno ingles
137	Hautbois d'amour	Oboe d'amore	Oboe d'amore	Oboe d'amore	Oboe d'amore
138	Hautboïste	Oboist	Oboista	Oboist	Oboísta
139	Clarinette	Clarinet	Clarinetto	Klarinette	Clarinete
140	Clarinettiste	Clarinettist Clarinetist	Clarinettista	Klarinettist	Clarinetista
141	Basson	Bassoon	Fagotto	Fagott	Fagote
142	Bassoniste	Bassoonist	Fagottista	Fagottist	Fagotista
143	Contre-basson	Contrabassoon	Contrafagotto	Kontrafagott	Contrafagote
144	Embouchure	Mouthpiece	Imboccatura Bocchino	Mundstück	Embocadura
145	Anche	Reed	Lingua Ancia	Blatt Blätchen	Lengüeta
146	Perce	Hole Key	Foro Buco	Löcher	Orificio
147	Sourdine	Mute	Sordina	Dämpfer	Sordina
148	Flûte à bec Flûte douce	Recorder	Flauto a becco Flauto dolce	Blockflöte	Flauta de pico Flauta dulce
149	Cromorne	Krummhorn	Cromorno	Krummhorn	Cromorno
150	Cornemuse	Bagpipe	Cornamusa	Dudelsack	Gaita
151	Cornemuse	Bagpipe	Zampogna	Dudelsack	Cornamusa
152	Fifre	Fife	Piffeto	Querpfeife	Flautín Pífano
153	Harmonica	Harmonica	Armonica	Mundharmonika	Armónica

N°	FRANCAIS	AMERICAN ENGLISH	ITALIANO	DEUTSCH	ESPAÑOL
154	Chalumeau	Chalumeau	Zampogna Cennamella	Schalmei	Caramillo
155	Harmonica à bouche	Harmonica Mouth organ	Armonica a bucca	Mundharmonika	Harmónica
156	Flageolet	Flageolet	Flautino	Flageolett	Caramillo
157	Cor de basset	Basset horn	Corno di bassetto	Bassethorn	Corno di bassetto
158	GROUPE DES CUIVRES	BRASS SECTION	OTTONI	BLECHINSTRU-MENTE	GRUPO DE METALES
159	Cor d'harmonie	Valve horn	Corno	Ventilhorn	Corno/Trompa
160	Corniste	Horn player	Cornista	Hornist	Cornista
161	Trompette	Trumpet	Tromba	Trompete	Trompeta
162	Trompettiste	Trumpet player	Trombetista Suonatore di tromba	Trompetist	Trompetista
163	Trompette basse	Bass trumpet	Tromba bassa	Basstrompete	Trompeta baja
164	Cornet	Cornet	Cornetta	Klaphörnchen	Corneta
165	Cornettiste	Cornet player	Cornettista	Klapphörnchen-spieler	Cornetista
166	Trombone	Trombone	Trombone	Posaune	Trombón
167	Trombone ténor	Tenor trombone	Trombone tenore	Tenorposaune	Trombón tenor
168	Trombone alto	Alto trombone	Trombone contralto	Altposaune	Trombón alto
169	Trombone basse	Bass trombone	Trombone basso	Bass posaune	Trombón bajo
170	Tromboniste	Trombonist	Trombonista	Posaunist	Trobonista
171	Tuba	Tuba	Tuba	Tuba	Tuba
172	Contre-tuba	Contrabass-tuba	Contratuba	Kontrabasstuba	Contratuba Tuba contrabajo
173	Tubiste	Tuba player	Tubista	Tubaspieler	Tubista
174	Saxophone	Saxophone	Sassofono	Saxophon	Saxofón
175	Saxophone soprano	Soprano saxophone	Sassofono soprano	Sopran-saxophon	Saxo soprano
176	Saxophone alto	Alto saxophone	Sassofono contralto	Altsaxophon	Saxo alto
177	Saxophone tenor	Tenor saxophone	Sassofono tenore	Tenorsaxophon	Saxo tenor
178	Saxophone baryton	Baritone saxophone	Sassofono baritono	Baritonsaxophon	Saxo barítono
179	Saxophone basse	Bass saxophone	Sassofono basso	Bass-saxophon	Saxo bajo

N°	FRANCAIS	AMERICAN ENGLISH	ITALIANO	DEUTSCH	ESPAÑOL
180	Sax-horn	Saxhorn	Sax horn Flicorno	Sax-horn Flügelhorn	Sax-horn
181	Saxophoniste	Saxophonist	Sassofonista	Saxophonist	Saxofonista
182	Bombarde	Shawm Bass shawm Bombardon	Bombarda	Pummer Brumbass	Bombarda
183	Bugle	Bugle Saxhorn	Flicorno	Signalhorn Flügelhorn	Flisocorno
184	Clairon	Bugle	Cornetta	Zinke	Corneta
185	Euphonium	Euphonium	Eufonio	Euphonium	Eufonio
186	Hélicon	Helicon Sousaphone	Bombardone Helicon	Helicon	Bombardón
187	Sarrusophone	Sarrusophone	Sarrusofono	Sarrusophon	Sarrusofón
188	Serpent	Serpent	Serpentone	Serpent Basshorn	Serpentón
189	Embouchure	Mouthpiece	Imboccatura Bocchino	Mundstück	Embocadura
190	Perce	Hole Key	Foro	Löcher	Orificio
191	Sourdine	Mute	Sordina	Dämpfer	Sordina
192	Coulisse	Slide	Coulisse Tiro	Zug Scheid Kulisse	Bomba
193	Piston	Valve	Pistone	Schubventil	Pistón
194	Pavillon	Bell	Padiglione	Schalltrichter	Pabellón
195	Son cuivré	Cuivré Brassy	Suono metallico "cuivré"	Geschmettert	Sonido abierto
196	Son bouché	Stopped (on the horn)	Suono Chiuso	Gestopft	Sonido cerrado Sonido tapado
197	PERCUSSIONS	PERCUSSION	PERCUSSIONE	SCHLAGWERK SCHLAGINSTRU-MENTE	INSTRUMENTOS DE PERCUSIÓN
198	Percussionniste	Percussionist	Percussionista	Schlagzeuger	Percusionista
199	Batterie	Percussion Battery Drums	Batteria	Schlagzeug	Batería
200	Batteur	Drummer	Batterista	Schlagzeuger	Baterista

N°	FRANCAIS	AMERICAN ENGLISH	ITALIANO	DEUTSCH	ESPAÑOL
201	INSTRUMENTS A SONS DETER-MINES	PITCHED INS-TRUMENTS	STRUMENTI A PERCUSSIONE DETERMINATA	INSTRUMENTE MIT BESTIMMTEN KLANGE	INSTRUMENTOS DETERMINADOS
202	Cloches	Bells	Campane	Glocken	Campanas
203	Cloches-tubes	Tubular bells	Campane tubolari	Röhrglocken	Campanas tubulares
204	Cloches-plaques	Plate bells	Campane di placche	Platteglocken	Campanas en placa
205	Jeu de cloches	Set of bells	Gruppo di campane	Glockenwerk	Juego de campanas
206	Cloches de vache	Cowbells	Campanaccio	Kuhglocken Alpenglocken	Cencerros
207	Célesta	Celesta	Celesta	Celesta	Celesta
208	Crotale	Crotale	Crotalo	Schellenbaum	Crótalo
209	Crotales	Crotales	Crotali	Kleine Tanzbecken	Crótalos
210	Jeu de timbres	Glockenspiel	Campanelli	Glockenspiel	Campanelli
211	Timbales	Kettledrums Timpani	Timpani	Pauke	Timbales
212	Timbalier	Timpanist	Timpanista	Paukenspieler	Timbalero
213	Roulement (de timbale)	Roll (of kettle drum)	Rullo	Paukenwirbel	Redoble Rulo
214	Métallophone	Metallophone	Metallofono	Metallophon	Metalófono
215	Marimbaphone	Marimbaphone	Xilorimba Silorimba	Marimbaphon	Xilorimba
216	Vibraphone	Vibraphone	Vibrafono	Vibraphon	Vibráfono
217	Vibraphoniste	Vibraphonist	Vibrafonista	Vibraphonist	Vibrafonista
218	Xylophone	Xylophone	Xilofono Silofono	Xylophon	Xilofón
219	Xylophoniste	Xylophonist	Xilofonista	Xylophonist	Xilofonista
220	Marimba	Marimba	Marimba	Marimba	Marimba
221	Glockenspiel	Glockenspiel	Campanelli Timbre Lira	Glockenspiel	Glockenspiel
222	INSTRUMENTS EN PEAU	MEMBRANO-PHONE	STRUMENTI DI PELLE	FELLINSTRU-MENTE	INSTRUMENTOS DE PIEL MEMBRANÓFONOS
223	Tambour	Drum	Tamburo	Trommel	Tambor
224	Tambour de basque	Tambourine	Tamburo basco Tamburino	Schëllentrommel	Tambor vasco
225	Tambourin	Tambourin	Tamburello	Tamburin	"Tambourin"
226	Tambour militaire	Side drum	Tamburo militare	Militärtrommel	Tambor militar

N°	FRANCAIS	AMERICAN ENGLISH	ITALIANO	DEUTSCH	ESPAÑOL
227	Tambour de bois	Log drum	Tamburo di legno	Schlitztrommel	Tambor de madera
228	Tambour à friction	String drum	Tamburo frottato	Reibtrommel	Tambor frotado
229	Tambourin à grelots	Tambourine	Tamburello a sona-gli	Schellentrommel	Cascabeles
230	Caisse claire	Snare drum	Cassa chiara	Kleine trommel Leinen trommel	Caja clara
231	Caisse claire sans timbre	Snare drum without snares	Cassa senza corda	Kleine trommel Ohne schqarrsaite	Caja sin cuerda
232	Caisse claire avec timbre	Snare drum with snares	Cassa colla corda	Kleine trommel Mit schnarrsaite	Caja con timbre
233	Caisse roulante	Tenor drum	Cassa rulante	Rollirtrommel Wirbeltrommel	Caja rolante
234	Grosse caisse	Bass drum	Gran cassa	Grosse trommel	Gran caja Bombo
235	Tom	Tom-tom	Tom-tom	Tom	Tom
236	Tam-tam	Tam-tam	Tam-tam	Tam-tam	Tam-tam
237	Tam-tam aigu	High tam-tam	Tam-tam acuto	Hohes tam-tam	Tam-tam agudo
238	Tam-tam grave	Low tam-tam	Tam-tam grave	Tiefes Tam-tam	Tam-tam grave
239	Tarole	"Pancake" Drum	Cassa chiara piccola	Kleine Militärtrommel	Redoblante
240	Bongo	Bongo	Bongo	Bongo	Bongó
241	Guimbarde	Jew's-harp	Scacciapensieri Guitarraccia	Brummeisen Maultrommel	Guimbarda Guitarrón
242	INSTRUMENTS A SONS INDE-TERMINES	UNPITCHED INSTRUMENTS	STRUMENTI A PERCUSSIONE INDETERMINATA	INSTRUMENTE MIT UNBESTIM-MTEN KLANGE	INSTRUMENTOS DE PERCUSION INDETERMINA-DOS
243	Bloc de bois	Wood block	Wood block Blocco di legno	Woodblock	"Cocos"
244	Cymbalum	Cymbalum	Zimbalon	Cymbal Hackbrett	Címbalón
245	Cymbales choquées	Choke cymbals	Piatti manuali	Gestossenes Becken	Platillos manuales
246	Cymbale chinoise	Chinese cymbal	Piatto cinese	Chinesisches Becken	Platillo chino
247	Cymbales suspendues	Suspended cymbals	Piatti sospesi	Freihängendes Becken	Platillos suspendidos
248	Cymbale turque	Turkish cymbal	Piatto turco	Türkisches becken	Platillo turco

N°	FRANCAIS	AMERICAN ENGLISH	ITALIANO	DEUTSCH	ESPAÑOL
249	"Charleston" Cymbale	High-hat cymbal	"Charleston"	Charleston becken	"Charleston"
250	Crécelle	Rattle	Raganella	Klapper	Maraca
251	Castagnettes	Castanets	Castagnette Nacchere	Castagnettes Kastagnette Tanzklappern	Castañuelas
252	Cymbale	Cymbal	Piatti	Becken	Platillo
253	Flûte à coulisse	Slide-whistle	Sirena di fischietto	Schiebe Flöte	Sirena de pico Silbato
254	Fouet	Whip Slapstick	Frusta	Rute	Látigo
255	Gong	Gong	Gong	Gong	Gong
256	Grelots	Sleigh bells	Sonagli Campanelli	Schellen	Cascabeles
257	Maracas	Maracas	Maracas	Maracas	Maracas
258	Sirène	Siren	Sirena	Sirene	Sirena
259	Scie musicale	Musical saw	Sega	Musikalische Säge	Serrucho
260	Sifflet	Whistle	Fischietto	Pfeife	Pito
261	Triangle	Triangle	Triangolo	Triangel	Triangulo
262	Baguettes	Drumsticks	Bacchette	Trommelstock Schlägel	Baquetas
263	Baguettes dures	Hard drumsticks	Bacchette Forte	Harter Schlägel	Baquetas duras
264	Baguettes de bois	Wooden drumsticks	Bacchette di legno	Holzschlägel	Baquetas duras
265	Baguettes d'éponge	Sponge-headed drumsticks	Bacchette di spugna	Schwammstab Schwammschlägel	Baquetas de esponja
266	Baguettes douces	Soft drumsticks	Bacchette sottile	Weicher schlägel	Baquetas blandas
267	Balais	Brush	Spazzolini	Schlägbesen Besen	Escobillas
268	Mailloche	Bass drumstick	Mazzuolo	Holzschlegel Paukenschlegel	Maza
269	CLAVIER	KEYBOARD	TASTIERA	TASTATUR KLAVIATUR	TECLADO
270	Piano	Piano	Pianoforte	Klavier	Piano
271	Pianiste	Pianist	Pianista	Pianist	Pianista
272	Piano droit	Upright piano	Piano verticale	Aufrechtstehendes Klavier	Piano vertical
273	Piano à queue	Grand piano	Piano a coda	Flügel Konzertflügel	Piano de cola

N°	FRANCAIS	AMERICAN ENGLISH	ITALIANO	DEUTSCH	ESPAÑOL
274	Table d'harmonie	Sound board	Tavola d'armonia	Resonanzboden	Tabla armonica Tabla de resonancia
275	Touche (Inst. à clavier)	Key of the piano	Tastiera	Taste	Teclado
276	Doigté	Fingering	Diteggiatura Tocco	Fingersatz	Digitación
277	Pédale	Pedal	Pedale	Pedal Fusstaste	Pedal
278	Etouffoir	Damper	Sordina	Schalldämpfer	Apagador Sordina
279	Clavecin	Harpsichord	Clavicembalo	Cembalo	Clavecín Clavicembalo Cémbalo
280	Claveciniste	Harpsichordist	Clavice Balista	Cembalist	Clavecinista Clavicembalista Cembalista
281	Harmonium	Harmonium	Organetto Harmonium	Harmonium Zimmerorgel	Armonio
282	Epinette	Spinet	Spinetta	Spinett	Espineta
283	Orgue	Organ	Organo	Orgel	Organo
284	Organiste	Organist	Organista	Organist Orgelspieler	Organista
285	Orgue positif	Positive organ	Organo positivo	Orgelpositiv	Organo positivo
286	Orgue de barbarie	Barrel organ	Organetto di barbaria	Drehorgel	Organo de barbarie
287	Registration	Registration	Registrazione	Registratur	Registración
288	Pieds (8, 16, etc.)	Foot Feet (8- foot stop, 16- foot stop, etc)	Piedi	Unterchormass	Pies (8, 16 etc.)
289	Accouplement (claviers)	Coupler	Accoppiamento	Manual Koppler Koppelung	Acoplamiento (Teclados)
290	Accouplement à l'octave	Octave coupler	Accoppiamento all' ottava	Oktavkoppel	Acoplamiento a la octava
291	Accouplement de pédalier	Pedal coupler	Accoppiamento de la pedaliera	Pedalkoppel	Acoplamiento a la pedal
292	Jeux d'orgue	Organ stop	Registri dell'organo	Orgelzug Orgelwerk	Juegos del organo Registros
293	Grand jeu	Full organ	Grande registro	Volles Werk	Gran juego
294	Jeu de mutation Mixtures	Mutation stop Mixture stop	Gioco de mutazione	Nebenstimme	Juego de mutación

N°	FRANCAIS	AMERICAN ENGLISH	ITALIANO	DEUTSCH	ESPAÑOL
295	Jeu de flûtes	Flute stop	Flauti	Flötenzug	Juego de flautas
296	Jeu d'anches	Reed stop	Ancie	Rohrwerk	Juegos de lengüetas
297	Tribune de l'orgue	Organ loft	Tribuna del'organo	Orgelchor	Coro Tribuna del organo
298	Pédalier	Pedal board	Pedaliera	Fussklavier	Pedalera
299	Fonds	Foundation stops	Principali	Prinzipal	Principal
300	Buffet (orgue)	Organ case	Cassa	Orgelhäuse Orgelkasten	Caja Pabellón
301	Soufflerie	Bellows	Soffieria	Gebläse	Trompetería
302	Tuyau d'orgue	Organ pipe	Canna d'organo	Orgelpfeife	Tubería del órgano
303	Voix céleste	Voix céleste Vox angelica	Voce celesta	Celesta Engelstimme	Voz celesta Voz celestial
304	Accordéon	Accordion	Accordeon Fisarmonica	Ziehharmonika Akkordeon	Acordeón
305	Accordéoniste	Accordeonist	Fisarmonicista	Akkordeonist	Acordeonista
306	Bandonéon	Bandoneon	Bandoneon	Bandoneon	Bandoneón
307	Bandonéoniste	Bandoneonist	Bandoneonista	Bandoneonist	Bandoneonista
308	Cistre allemand	German zither	Pandora	Pandora	Pandora
309	Cistre à clavier	Keyboard zither	Cetra a tastiera	Tastencister	Cistro
310	GROUPE DES CORDES	STRING SECTION	ARCHI	STREICHINSTRU-MENTE STREICHER	GRUPO DE CUERDAS
311	Cordes frottées	Bowed-string instruments	Frottate	Gestrichen	Cuerdas frotadas
312	Violon	Violin	Violino	Geige Violin	Violín
313	Violoniste	Violinist	Violinista	Violinist	Violinista
314	Premiers violons	First violins	Primi violini	Ersten Geigen	Primeros Violines
315	Seconds violons	Second violins	Secondi violini	Zweiten Geigen	Segundos violines
316	Alto	Viola	Viola	Bratsche Viola	Viola
317	Altiste	Violist	Violista	Bratschist	Violista
318	Violoncelle	Cello	Violoncello	Cello	Violonchelo
319	Violoncelliste	Cellist	Violoncellista	Cellist	Violonchelista
320	Contrebasse	Double bass	Contrabasso	Kontrabass	Contrabajo

N°	FRANCAIS	AMERICAN ENGLISH	ITALIANO	DEUTSCH	ESPAÑOL
321	Contrebassiste	Double bass player	Contrabassista	Kontrabassist	Contrabajista
322	Corde	String	Corda	Saite	Cuerda
323	Chanterelle	Cantino Highest string	Prima (corda)	Singsaite Quinte	Prima (cuerda)
324	Cordier	Tailpiece	Cordiera	Saitenbrett	Cordal
325	Ame	Sound post	Anima	Stimmholz	Alma
326	Chevalet	Bridge	Ponticello	Steg	Puente
327	Manche	Fingerboard	Manico	Hals	Mango
328	Archet	Bow	Arco	Bogen	Arco
329	Coup d'archet	Bow stroke	Colpo d'arco	Bogenstrich	Golpe de arco
330	Tiré	Down-bow	Trascinare	Abstrich	Tirado
331	Poussé	Up-bow	Spinto	Gestossen Aufstrich	Empujado
332	Crin de l'archet	Bowhair	Crini dell'arco	Rosshaar	Crin del arco
333	Bois de l'archet	Wood of the bow	Legno	Bogenholz	Madera del arco
334	Talon de l'archet	Nut of the bow Heel Frog	Tallone dell'arco	Am frosch	Talón
335	Boîte à violon	Violin case	Scatola di violino	Violinkasten	Estuche
336	Sourdine	Mute	Sordina	Dämpfer	Sordina
337	Martelé	Hammered	Martellatto	Gehämmert	"Martellatto"
338	Sautillé	Saltando Spiccato	Saltellatto	Kurz Gestosen und betont	"Saltellatto"
339	Doubles cordes	Double stops	Doppie corde	Doppelgriff	Dobles cuerdas
340	A la corde	Alla corda	Alla corda	An der saite Alla corda	"alla corda"
341	Viole de gambe	Viola da gamba	Viola da gamba	Gambe Kniegeige	Viola da gamba
342	Gambiste	Viola da gamba player	Suonatore di viola da gamba	Gambist	Gambista
343	Viole d'amour	Viola d'amore	Viola d'amore	Liebesgeige	Viola de amor
344	Par-dessus de viole	Descant viol	Sopra la viola	Damengeige	Por sobre la viola
345	Bassiste	Bass player	Bassista	Bassist	Bajista
346	Cordes pincées	Plucked string instruments	Corde pizzicate	Gekniffen	Cuerdas punteadas Cuerdas pellizcadas

N°	FRANCAIS	AMERICAN ENGLISH	ITALIANO	DEUTSCH	ESPAÑOL
347	Harpe	Harp	Arpa	Harfe	Arpa
348	Harpiste	Harpist	Arpista	Harfist	Arpista
349	Table d'harmonie	Sound board	Tavola d'armonia	Resonanzboden	Tabla de resonancia
350	Guitare	Guitar	Chitarra	Gitarre	Guitarra
351	Guitariste	Guitarist	Chitarrista	Gitarrist	Guitarrista
352	Rosace	Sound hole	Rosa	Stern	Roseta
353	Touche (Inst. à cordes)	Fingerboard	Tasta	Griff	Diapasón
354	Cheville	Peg (Tuning)	Caviglia	Wirbel	Clavija
355	Sillet	Nut	Capotasto	Sattel	Capodasto Ceja
356	Doigté	Fingering	Diteggiatura	Fingersatz	Digitación
357	Démancher	To shift (The hand position)	"Smanicare"	Demanchieren	Demancher
358	Plectre	Plectrum	Plettro	Plektrum	Plectro
359	Médiator	Pick	Plettro	Plektrum	Plectro
360	Luth	Lute	Liuto	Laute	Laúd
361	Cithare	Kithara	Lira	Zither	Cítara
362	Mandoline	Mandolin	Mandolino	Mandola	Mandolina
363	Cistre-théorbe	Double-necked guitar Double-necked lute	Cistre tiorbato	Ercister	Cítara-theorba
364	Psaltérion	Psaltery Zither	Salterio	Psalter	Salterio
365	Lyre	Lyre	Lira Cetra	Leier	Lira
366	Cistre	Cittern	Cetra	Cister	Cistro
367	MUSIQUE ANCIENNE	EARLY MUSIC	MUSICA ANTICA	ALTERE MUSIK	MÚSICA ANTIGUA
368	Trope	Trope	Cantilena	Tropus	Cantilena
369	Passage	Passage	Passaggio	Stelle Passage	Redobles
370	Neumes	Neumes	Neumi	Neumen	Neumas
371	Déchant	Descant	Discanto	Gegenstimme	Discanto
372	Bicinium	Bicinium	Bicinium	Zweistimmiger Satz	Bicinio

N°	FRANCAIS	AMERICAN ENGLISH	ITALIANO	DEUTSCH	ESPAÑOL
373	Tricinium	Tricinium	Tricinium	Dreistimmiger Satz	Tricinio
374	MUSIQUE BAROQUE	BAROQUE MUSIC	MUSICA BAROCCA	BAROK MUSIK	MÚSICA BARROCA
375	MUSIQUE CONTEMPO-RAINE	CONTEMPO-RARY MUSIC	MUSICA CONTEMPO-RANEA	MODERNE MUSIK	MÚSICA CONTEMPO-RÁNEA
376	Dodécaphonisme	12-tone music Dodecaphonic music	Dodecafonismo	Zwölftontechnik	Dodecafonismo
377	Série	Series	Serie	Reihe	Serie
378	MUSIQUE DE CHAMBRE	CHAMBER MUSIC	MUSICA DA CAMERA	KAMMERMUSIK	MÚSICA DE CÁMARA
379	Orchestre de chambre	Chamber orchestra	Orchestra da camera	Kammerorchester	Orquesta de cámara
380	Ensemble Instrumental	Instrumental ensemble	Complesso strumentale	Ensemble	Conjunto instrumental
381	Duo	Duo	Duo	Duett	Dúo
382	Trio	Trio	Trio	Trio	Trío
383	Trio d'anches	Trio for reed instruments Wind trio	Trio di ance	Bläsertrio	Trío de lengüetas
384	Quatuor	Quartet	Quartetto	Quartett	Cuarteto
385	Quatuor à cordes	String quartet	Quartetto classico	Streichquartett	Cuarteto de cuerdas
386	Quintette	Quintet	Quintetto	Quintett	Quinteto
387	Quintette à vent	Wind quintet	Quintetto per fiati	Bläserquintett	Quinteto de vientos
388	Sextuor	Sextet	Sestetto	Sextet	Sexteto
389	Septuor	Septet	Settimino	Septett	Septeto Septimino
390	Octuor	Octet	Ottetto	Oktett	Octeto
391	Octuor de cuivres	Brass octet	Ottetto di ottoni	Blechoktett	Octeto de cobres Octeto de metales
392	Obligé	Obbligato	Obbligato	Obligat	Obligado
393	INSTRUMENTS ELECTRONI-QUES	ELECTRONIC INSTRUMENTS	STRUMENTI ELETTRONICI	ELEKTRONISCHEN INSTRUMENTE	INSTRUMENTOS ELECTRÓNICOS
394	Guitare électrique	Electric guitar	Chitarra elettrica	Elektrische gitarre	Guitarra eléctrica
395	Guitare basse	Bass guitar	Chitarra bassa	Bassgitarre	Guitarra baja Bajo

N°	FRANCAIS	AMERICAN ENGLISH	ITALIANO	DEUTSCH	ESPAÑOL
396	Générateur de sons	Sound generator	Generatore	Generator (zur Erzeugung elektrischer schwin gungen)	Generador de sonido
397	Orgue électrique	Electronic organ	Organo elettronico	Elektronische orgel	Organo electrónico
398	Ondes Martenot	Ondes Martenot	Onde Martenot	Ondes Martenot	Ondas Martenot
399	Ondiste	Ondes Martenot player	Suonatore di onde Martenot	Ondes Martenot spieler	Ondista
400	Oscillateur	Oscillator	Oscillatore	Schwankung	Oscilador
401	Piano électrique	Electric piano	Pianoforte elettronico	Elektroklavier Elektronisches Klavier	Piano electrónico
402	Synthétiseur	Synthesizer	Sintetizzatore	Synthesizer	Sintetizador
403	Disque	Record	Disco	Schallplatte	Disco
404	Cassette	Cassette	Cassette	Kassette	Cassette Magasin
405	Sillon	Groove	Solco	Rille (Des schneidstichels in der schall Platte)	Surco
406	Microsillon	Microgroove	Microsolco	Langspielplatte	Microsurco
407	Plage (sur disque)	Band	Banda sonora	Tonband	Surco
408	Tourne-disque	Turntable	Giradischi	Plattenteller	Giradiscos
409	Electrophone	Record player	Giradischi	Elektrophon	Tocadiscos Pasadiscos Giradiscos
410	Lecture	Needle and Cartridge	Lettura	Magnettonabtaster	Lectura Lector magnético
411	Bras de lecture	Tone arm	Braccio	Tonabnehmer-arm Tonarm	Brazo de lectura
412	Aiguille	Needle Stylus	Puntina	Tonabnehmer	Aguja
413	Amplificateur	Amplifier	Amplificatore	Schallplattenverstärker Lautverstärker Tonverstärker	Amplificador
414	Haut-parleur	Loudspeaker	Cassa acustica Altoparlante	Lautsprecher	Altoparlante
415	Monophonie	Monophonic Mono	Monofonia	Einstimmigkeit	Monofonía

N°	FRANCAIS	AMERICAN ENGLISH	ITALIANO	DEUTSCH	ESPAÑOL
416	Stéréophonie	Stereophonic Stereo	Stereofonia	Stereophonie Raumklang	Estereofonía
417	Quadriphonie	Quadraphonic	Cuadrofonia	Quadraphon	Cuadrafonía
418	Multiphonie	Multiphonic	Multifonia	Mehrkanalig	Multifonía
419	Enregistrement	Recording	Registrazione	Aufnahme	Grabación
420	Ingénieur du son	Sound engineer	Ingegnere di suono	Ton ingenieur	Ingeniero de sonido Técnico de sonido
421	Prise de son	Recording (by microphone)	Pressa di suono	Tonaufnahme	Toma de sonido
422	Montage	Montage Splicing Editing	Montaggio	Montage	Montaje
423	Mixage	Mixing	Miscela	Ton Mischung	Mezcla
424	Microphone	Microphone	Microfono	Mikrophon	Micrófono
425	Bidirectionnel	Bi-directional	Bidirezionale	Zweiseitig gerichtetes Mikrophon	Micrófono bidireccional
426	Micro de contact	Contact microphone	Microcontatto	Kontaktmikrophon	Micrófono de contacto
427	Chambre d'écho	Echo chamber	Camera d'eco	Hallraum	Cámara de eco
428	Echo	Echo	Eco	Echo	Eco
429	Réverbération	Reverberation	Riverberazione	Nachhall	Reverberación
430	Magnétophone	Tape recorder	Registratore	Magnettongerät Tonbandgerät	Grabador Magnetófono
431	Bande magnétique	Magnetic tape	Nastro magnetico	Magnettonband	Banda magnética Cinta magnética
432	Piste	Track	Pista	Tonspur	Pista Banda
433	Bande de son	Sound recording tape	Banda di suono	Tonstreifen	Banda de sonido
434	Multi-pistes	Multi-track	Multipiste	Mehrspürig	Multipista Play-back
435	Surimpression	Overdub	Sovra impressione	Obereinanderstellung	Sobreimpresión Play-back Replay
436	Gravure (de disque)	Cutting (records)	Incisione	Kanzelle Register kanzelle	Matrizado Prensado Grabación
437	Electro-acoustique	Electro-acoustic	Elettroacustica	Elektroakustik	Electroácustica

N°	FRANCAIS	AMERICAN ENGLISH	ITALIANO	DEUTSCH	ESPAÑOL
438	Aigus	Highs Treble	Acuti	Höhen	Agudos
439	Boucle	Loop	Anello di nastro	(Tonband) Schleife	Rulo Boucle
440	Bruit blanc	White noise	Rumore bianco Suono bianco	Weisses Rauschen	Ruido blanco Sonido blanco
441	Bruit "rose"	Pink noise	Rumore "rosa"	Rosa Rauschen	Ruido rosa Sonido rosa
442	Bruit de fond	Background noise	Rumore di fondo	Geräuschkulisse	Ruido de fondo
443	Continu	Continuous	Continuo	Ununterbrochen	Continuado
444	Densité	Density	Densità	Schalldichte	Densidad
445	Discontinu	Discontinuous	Discontinuo	Unterbrochen	Discontinuo
446	Emission du son	Sound emission	Emissione del suono	Tonsendung	Emisión del sonido
447	Entrée	Input	Ingresso	Eingang	Entrada
448	Filtre	Filter	Filtro	Klangfilter	Filtro
449	Formant	Formant	Formativo	Formant	Formante
450	Graves	Lows	Gravi	Tiefen	Graves
451	Longueur d'onde	Wave-length	Lunghezza d'onda	Wellenlänge	Largo de onda
452	Niveau	Level	Livello	Hörschwelle Tonstärke	Nivel
453	Noeud	Node	Nodo	Schwingungsknoten	Nudo
454	Onde	Wave	Onda	Welle	Onda
455	Partiel	Partial	Parziale	Einzeln	Parcial
456	Période	Period	Periodo	Periode	Período
457	Propagation du son	Propagation of sound	Propagazione del suono	Tonausbreitung	Propagación del sonido
458	Résonance	Resonance	Risonanza	Widerhallen	Resonancia
459	Résonateur	Resonator	Risonatore	Resonator	Resonador
460	Saturation	Saturation Overload	Saturazzione	Ubersteuerung	Saturación
461	Sinusoïdale (onde)	Sine wave	Onda sinusoidale	Sinuswelle	Onda sinusoidal
462	Sortie	Output	Uscità	Ausgang	Salida
463	Souffle	Background noise	Soffio	Rausch	Soplo Ruido de fondo

N°	FRANCAIS	AMERICAN ENGLISH	ITALIANO	DEUTSCH	ESPAÑOL
464	Synchronisation	Synchronization	Sincronizzazione	Synchronisierung	Sincronización
465	Ventre	Antinode	Ventre	Schwingungsbauch	Ensanche Vientre
466	Vibration	Vibration	Vibrazione	Schwingung	Vibración
467	CONCERT	CONCERT	CONCERTO	KONZERT	CONCIERTO
468	Concertiste	Player	Concertista	Konzertist Konzertgeber	Concertista
469	Virtuose	Virtuoso	Virtuoso	Virtuos	Virtuoso
470	Récital	Recital	Recitale	Abend Liederabend Klavierabend	Recital
471	Festival	Festival	Festival	Festpiel	Festival
472	Répétition	Rehearsal	Prova	Probe	Ensayo
473	Répétiteur	Rehearsal coach	Maestro concertatore	Repetitor	Maestro de ensayo
474	Assistant	Assistant	Assistente	Assistent	Asistente
475	Salle de concert	Concert hall	Sala Aula	Konzertraum Konzertsaal	Sala de conciertos
476	Administrateur	Administrator	Amministratore	Konzertverwalter	Administrador Empresario
477	Organisateur de concert	Concert organizer Impresario	Organizzatore di concerti	Konzertverwalter	Organizador de conciertos Empresario
478	OPERA	OPERA	OPERA	OPER	OPERA
479	Opéra comique	Comic opera	Opera comica	Komische Oper	Opera cómica
480	Opéra bouffe	Opera buffa	Opera buffa	Buffo-oper	Opera bufa
481	Opérette	Operetta	Operetta	Operette	Opereta
482	Scène	Stage	Scena	Szene	Escena
483	Musique de Scène	Music for the theatre	Musica di scena	Bühnenmusik	Música de escena
484	Acte	Act	Atto	Aufzug	Acto
485	Régisseur	Stage director	Regista	Régisseur	Director de escena
486	Metteur en scène	Director	Regista	Régisseur Spielbeiter	Director de escena
487	Ténor wagnérien	Wagnerian tenor Helden tenor	Tenore wagneriano	Heldentenor	Tenor wagneriano

N°	FRANCAIS	AMERICAN ENGLISH	ITALIANO	DEUTSCH	ESPAÑOL
488	Doublure	Doubling	Contrafigura	Verdopplung	Suplente Doble
489	Administrateur	Administrator	Ammisnistratore	Konzertverwalter	Administrador Empresario
490	DANSE	DANCE	DANZA	TANZ	DANZA
491	Ballet	Ballet	Balletto Ballo	Ballett	Ballet Baile Danza
492	Pas de quatre	Quartet (ballet)	Passo di quatro	Quadratschritt Tanzschritt	Paso a cuatro
493	Quadrille	Quadrille	Quadriglia	Contretanz Quadrille	Contradanza
494	Danseur Danseuse	Dancer	Danzatore Danzatrice	Tänzer Tänzerin	Bailarín Bailarina
495	Ballerine	Ballerina	Ballerina	Ballettänzerin	Bailarina
496	Corps de ballet	Ballet company	Corpo di ballo	Ballettruppe	Cuerpo de baile
497	Chorégraphe	Choreographer	Coreografo	Choréograph	Coreógrafo
498	Maître de ballet	Ballet master Leader	Maestro di ballo	Balletmeister	Maestro de baile
499	Branle, Bransle	Brawl	Brando	Rundtanz	Branle
500	Balance	Balance	Equilibrio	Schaukeln Schwankung	Balance
501	CONSERVA-TOIRE	CONSERVA-TORY	CONSERVA-TORIO	KONSERVA-TORIUM	CONSERVA-TORIO
502	Solfège	Solfège	Solfeggio	Solfeggio	Solfeo
503	Solfier	To sing with solfège syllables	Solfeggiare	Solfeggieren	Solfear
504	Déchiffrer	To sight-read	Decifrare	Vom blatt lesen	Lectura a primera vista
505	Dictée musicale	Musical dictation	Dettato musicale	Musikdiktat	Dictado musical
506	THEORIE MUSICALE	MUSIC THEORY	TEORIA DELLA MUSICA	MUSIKTHEORIE	TEORIA DE LA MÚSICA
507	Portée	Staff	Pentagramma	Notenzeile Notenlinien Notenleiter	Pentagrama
508	Ligne	Line	Linea	Linie Zeile	Línea
509	Interligne	Space	Spazio	Zwischenzeile	Espacio

N°	FRANCAIS	AMERICAN ENGLISH	ITALIANO	DEUTSCH	ESPAÑOL
510	Ligne supplémentaire	Ledger lines	Linea addizionale	Beigefügte linie	Línea adicional
511	Clef Clé	Clef	Chiave	Schlüssel	Clave
512	Clef de sol	G clef Treble clef	Chiave di sol Chiave di violino	Violinschlüssel	Clave de sol
513	Clef d'ut	C clef	Chiave di do	Altschlüssel	Clave de do
514	Clef de fa	F clef Bass clef	Chiave di fa	Bass-schlüssel	Clave de fa
515	Notes	Notes	Note	Noten	Notas
516	Gamme	Scale	Scala	Skala	Escala
517	Ut Do	C Do	Do	C	Do
518	Ré	D Re	Re	D	Re
519	Mi	E Mi	Mi	E	Mi
520	Fa	F Fa	Fa	F	Fa
521	Sol	G Sol	Sol	G	Sol
522	La	A La	La	A	La
523	Si	B Si (Ti)	Si	H	Si
524	Altération	Alteration	Accidente	Alterierung	Alteración
525	Accident	Accidental	Accidente	Akzident	Accidente
526	Altération accidentelle	Alteration by accidental	Alterazione accidentale	Nebenvorzeichnung	Alteración Accidental
527	Dièse	Sharp	Diesis	Kreuz	Sostenido
528	Do dièse	C sharp	Do diesis	C is	Do sostenido
529	Ré dièse	D sharp	Re diesis	D is	Re sostenido
530	Mi dièse	E sharp	Mi diesis	E is	Mi sostenido
531	Fa dièse	F sharp	Fa diesis	F is	Fa sostenido
532	Sol dièse	G sharp	Sol diesis	G is	Sol sostenido
533	La dièse	A sharp	La diesis	A is	La sostenido
534	Si dièse	B sharp	Si diesis	H is	Si sostenido
535	Bémol	Flat	Bemolle	B e	Bemol

N°	FRANCAIS	AMERICAN ENGLISH	ITALIANO	DEUTSCH	ESPAÑOL
536	Do bémol	C flat	Do bemolle	C es	Do bemol
537	Ré bémol	D flat	Re bemolle	D es	Re bemol
538	Mi bémol	E flat	Mi bemolle	E s	Mi bemol
539	Fa bémol	F flat	Fa bemolle	F es	Fa bemol
540	Sol bémol	G flat	Sol bemolle	G es	Sol bemol
541	La bémol	A flat	La bemolle	A s	La bemol
542	Si bémol	B flat	Si bemolle	B	Si bemol
543	Double-dièse	Double sharp	Doppio diesis	Doppelkreuz	Doble sostenido
544	Do double-dièse	C double-sharp	Do doppio diesis	C isis	Do doble sostenido
545	Ré double-dièse	D double-sharp	Re doppio diesis	D isis	Re doble sostenido
546	Mi double-dièse	E double-sharp	Mi doppio diesis	E isis	Mi doble sostenido
547	Fa double-dièse	F double-sharp	Fa doppio diesis	F isis	Fa doble sostenido
548	Sol double-dièse	G double-sharp	Sol doppio diesis	G isis	Sol doble sostenido
549	La double-dièse	A double-sharp	La doppio diesis	A isis	La doble sostenido
550	Si double-dièse	B double-sharp	Si doppio diesis	H isis	Si doble sostenido
551	Double-bémol	Double-flat	Doppio bemolle	Doppelbe	Doble bemol
552	Do double-bémol	C double-flat	Do doppio bemolle	C eses	Do doble bemol
553	Ré double-bémol	D double-flat	Re doppio bemolle	D eses	Re doble bemol
554	Mi double-bémol	E double-flat	Mi doppio bemolle	E eses	Mi doble bemol
555	Fa double-bémol	F double-flat	Fa doppio bemolle	F eses	Fa doble bemol
556	Sol double-bémol	G double-flat	Sol doppio bemolle	G eses	Sol doble bemol
557	La double-bémol	A double-flat	La doppio bemolle	A eses	La doble bemol
558	Si double-bémol	B double-flat	Si doppio bemolle	H eses	Si doble bemol
559	Bécarre	Natural	Bequadro	Auflösungszeichen	Becuadro
560	Intervalle	Interval	Intervallo	Intervall Tonstufe	Intervalo
561	Ton	Tone Whole step	Tono	Ton	Tono
562	Demi-ton	Semi-tone	Semitono	Halbton	Semitono
563	Chromatique	Chromatic	Cromatico	Chromatisch	Cromático
564	Diatonique	Diatonic	Diatonico	Diatonisch Stufentönig	Diatónico
565	Micro-intervalle	Micro-interval	Microintervallo	Das kleinste interval	Microintervalo
566	Quart de ton	Quarter tone	Quarto di tono	Viertelton	Cuarto de tono
567	Tiers de ton	Third tone	Terzo di tono	Drittelton	Tercio de tono

N°	FRANCAIS	AMERICAN ENGLISH	ITALIANO	DEUTSCH	ESPAÑOL
568	Unisson	Unison	Unisono	Einklang	Unísono
569	Seconde	Second	Seconda	Sekunde	Segunda
570	Tierce	Third	Terza	Terz	Tercera
571	Quarte	Fourth	Quarta	Quart	Cuarta
572	Triton	Tritone	Tritono	Tritonus	Tritono
573	Quinte	Fifth	Quinta	Quint	Quinta
574	Sixte	Sixth	Sesta	Sext	Sexta
575	Septième	Seventh	Settima	Sept Septime	Séptima
576	Octave	Octave	Ottava	Oktav	Octava
577	Neuvième	Ninth	Nona	None	Novena
578	Dixième	Tenth	Decima	Dezime	Décima
579	Onzième	Eleventh	Undecima	Undezime	Oncena
580	Majeur	Major	Maggiore	Dur	Mayor
581	Mineur	Minor	Minore	Moll	Menor
582	Juste	Just	Giusto	Rein	Justa(o)
583	Augmenté	Augmented	Aumentato	Obermässig	Aumentado
584	Diminué	Diminished	Diminuito	Vermindert	Disminuído
585	Degré	Degree	Grado	Stufe	Grado
586	Tonique	Tonic Key note	Tonica	Tonika Grundton	Tónica
587	Sus-tonique	Supertonic	Sopratonica	Obertonica	Supertónica
588	Médiante	Mediant	Mediante	Mediante	Mediante
589	Sous-dominante	Subdominant	Sottodominante	Unterdominante	Subdominante
590	Dominante	Dominant	Dominante	Dominante	Dominante
591	Sus-dominante	Submediant Superdominant	Soppraddominante	Subdominante	Superdominante
592	Sensible	Leading tone	Sensibile	Leitton	Sensible
593	Tétracorde	Tetrachord	Tetracordo	Tetrachord	Tetracorde
594	Notation	Notation	Scrittura Notazione	Notierung	Escritura Notación
595	Figuration	Figuration	Figurazione	Figuration	Figuración
596	Solfège	Solfège	Solfeggio	Solfeggio Noten	Solfeo
597	Notation carrée	Square notation	Notazione quadrata	Quadratnotation	Notación cuadrada

N°	FRANCAIS	AMERICAN ENGLISH	ITALIANO	DEUTSCH	ESPAÑOL
598	Note carrée	Double whole note Breve	Nota quadrata	Brevis Doppeltaktnote Quadratnote	Cuadrada
599	Figures de notes	Note-shapes	Figure delle note	Notenfiguren	Figuras de nota
600	Signes musicaux	Musical signs	Segni musicali	Musikalischen Zeichen	Signos musicales
601	Valeurs de durée	Durational values	Valori di durata	Notendauer Notenwert	Valores de duración
602	Ronde	Whole note Semibreve	Breve	Ganze note	Redonda
603	Blanche	Half note Minim	Semibreve	Halbe note	Blanca
604	Noire	Quarter note Crotchet	Minima	Viertelnote	Negra
605	Croche	Eighth note Quaver	Semiminima	Achtelnote	Corchea
606	Double-croche	Sixteenth note Semiquaver	Croma	Sechzehntelnote	Semicorchea
607	Triple-croche	Thirty-second note Demisemiquaver	Semicroma	Zweiunddreissigs telnote	Fusa
608	Quadruple-croche	Sixty-fourth note Hemidemisemi- quaver	Biscroma	Vierundsechsigs- telnote	Semifusa
609	Silence	Rest	Pausa	Ruhezeichen Pausa	Silencio
610	Pause	Whole rest	Pausa di breve	Ganze pause	Silencio de redonda
611	Demi-pause	Half-rest	Pausa di semibreve	Halbe pause	Silencio de blanca
612	Soupir	Quarter rest	Pausa di minima	Viertel pause	Silencio de negra
613	Demi-soupir	Eighth rest	Pausa di semiminima	Achtel pause	Silencio de corchea
614	Quart de soupir	Sixteenth rest	Pausa di croma	Sechzehntel	Silencio de semicorchea
615	Huitième de soupir	Thirty-second rest	Pausa di semicroma	Zweiunddreissigstel Pause	Silencio de fusa
616	Seizième de soupir	Sixty-fourth rest	Pausa di biscroma	Vierundsechsigstel Pause	Silencio de semifusa
617	Duolet	Duplet	Duina	Duole	Dosillo
618	Triolet	Triplet	Terzina	Triole	Tresillo
619	Quartolet	Quadruplet	Quartina	Quartole	Cuatrillo

N°	FRANCAIS	AMERICAN ENGLISH	ITALIANO	DEUTSCH	ESPAÑOL
620	Quintolet	Quintuplet	Quintina	Quintole	Quintillo
621	Sextolet	Sextuplet	Sestina	Sextole	Seisillo
622	Septolet	Septuplet	Settimina	Septole	Heptasillo Sietesillo
623	Accolade	Brace	Grappa	Verbindungszug	Corchete
624	Point	Dot	Punto	Punkt	Puntillo
625	Note pointée	Dotted note	Nota puntata	Punktierte note	Nota con puntillo Figura con puntillo
626	Double point	Double dot	Doppio punto	Doppelpunkt	Doble puntillo
627	Liaison	Tie (over metric division) Slur (legato)	Legatura	Bindestrich Bindezeichen	Ligadura a) de prolongación b) de expresión
628	Ligatures	Beams Ligatures	Legatura	Bindebogen Ligaturen	Ligaduras
629	Ligature	Beam Ligature	Legatura	Bindebogen Ligatur	Ligadura
630	Rythme	Rhythm	Ritmo	Rhytmus	Ritmo
631	Valeur rythmique	Rythmic value	Valore ritmico	Rhytmuswert	Valor rítmico
632	Syncope	Syncopation	Sincopa	Synkope	Síncopa
633	Temps	Beat Tempo	Tempo	Taktteil	Tiempo Tempo
634	Métrique	Metric	Metrica	Metrik	Métrica
635	Métronome	Metronome	Metronomo	Metronom Taktmesser	Metrónomo
636	Indication Métronomique	Metronome mark	Indicazione metronomica	Metronomzahl Metronombezeichnung	Indicación metronómica
637	Mesure	Measure	Battuta Misura	Takt	Compás
638	Mesure simple	Simple (meter) Measure in...	Battuta semplice	Einfacher takt	Compás simple
639	Mesure composée	Compound meter	Battuta composta	Zusammengestzter Takt	Compás compuesto
640	Mesure binaire	Binary meter	Misura binaria	Zweiteiliger takt	Compás binario
641	Mesure ternaire	Ternary meter	Misura ternaria	Dreiteiliger takt	Compás ternario
642	Alla breve	Cut time	Alla breve	Allabrevetakt	Alla breve Compás de compasillo

N°	FRANCAIS	AMERICAN ENGLISH	ITALIANO	DEUTSCH	ESPAÑOL
643	Division binaire	Binary division	Misura binaria	Zweizählige Teilung	División binaria
644	Division ternaire	Ternary division	Misura ternaria	Dreizählige Teilung	División ternaria
645	Changement de mesure	Change of time	Cambio di misura	Taktveränderung	Cambio de compás
646	Barre de mesure	Bar	Sbarra	Taktstrich	Barra de compás
647	Double barre de mesure	Double bar	Doppia sbarra	Doppeltaktstrich	Doble barra
648	Point d'orgue	Pause Hold Fermata	Corona	Fermate	Calderón
649	Point d'arrêt	Pause on a rest	Corona sull'silenzio	Ruhezeichen Pause Fermata	Gran Pausa Calderón sobre silencio
650	Battement	Beat	Battimento	Taktschlag	Batimiento
651	Battre la mesure	To beat time	Battere la battuta	Taktieren den Takt Schlagen	Marcar del compás
652	Battue	Beat	Battuta	Taktschlag	Batimiento
653	Mouvement	Movement Tempo	Movimento	Bewegung	Movimiento Tempo
654	Contretemps	Off the beat	Contratempo	Zwischentakt	Contratiempo
655	Temps strié	Measured	Tempo controllato	Zeitmässig	Tiempo controlado
656	Temps lisse	Unmeasured	Tempo libero	Unzeitmässig	Tiempo libre
657	A deux temps	Of two beats (double time)	A due tempi	Zweivierteltaktig	A dos tiempos
658	Temps fort	Strong beat	Tempo forte	Schwerer Taktteil	Tiempo fuerte
659	Temps faible	Weak beat	Tempo debole	Leichter Taktteil	Tiempo debil
660	Levée du temps	Up-beat	Levare	Vorausschlagen Vorschlagen	"Elevar" "Levare"
661	Anacrouse	Anacrusis	Anacrusi	Anakrusis Auftakt	Anacrusa
662	Ornement	Ornament	Abbellimenti	Ornament	Adorno Ornamento
663	Abréviation	Abbreviation	Abbreviatura Abbreviazzione	Abkürzung	Abreviatura
664	Acciacature	Acciaccatura	Acciaccatura	Zusammenschlag (Vorschlag)	Acciacatura Acachatura

N°	FRANCAIS	AMERICAN ENGLISH	ITALIANO	DEUTSCH	ESPAÑOL
665	Agrément	Ornament Embellishment	Abbellimento	Ornamentirung	Agregado
666	Appogiature	Appoggiatura	Appoggiatura	Vorschlag	Apoyatura
667	Fioriture	Embellishment	Fioritura	Verzierung	Adorno Floritura
668	Grupetto	Ornament	Gruppetto	Gruppetto	Grupeto
669	Mordant	Mordent	Mordente	Mordant Pralltriller	Mordente
670	Petites notes	Grace notes	Piccole note	Stichnoten	Notas de adorno Notas fuera del tiempo Pequeñas notas
671	Trille	Trill	Trillo	Triller	Trino
672	Mode	Mode	Modo	Modus Kirchentonart	Modo
673	Dorien	Dorian	Dorico	Dorisch	Dórico
674	Hypodorien	Hypodorian	Ipodorico	Hypodorisch	Hipodórico
675	Lydien	Lydian	Lidio	Lidisch	Lidio
676	Mixolydien	Mixolydian	Missolidio	Mixolidisch	Mixolidio
677	Phrygien	Phrygian	Frigio	Phygisch	Frigio
678	Eolien	Aeolian	Eolico	Aolisch	Eólico
679	Ionien	Ionian	Ionico	Ionisch	Jónico
680	Modes ecclésiastiques	Ecclesiastical modes	Modi ecclesiastici	Kirchentonarten	Modos eclesiásticos
681	Gamme pentatonique	Pentatonic scale	Scala pentatonica	Pentatonische skala	Escala pentatonica
682	Gamme par tons	Whole-tone scale	Scala per toni	Ganztonskala	Escala por tonos
683	Chromatisme	Chromaticism	Cromatismo	Chromatik	Cromatismo
684	Diatonisme	Diatonicism Pan-diatonicism	Diatonismo	Diatonik	Diatonismo
685	Faux	Incorrect False Out of tune	Falso	Falsch	Falso
686	Mélodie	Song Lied	Melodia	Melodie	Melodía
687	Apotome	Apotome	Apotema	Apotome	Apótoma
688	Anapeste	Anapest	Anapesta	Anapäst Versfuss	Anapeste

N°	FRANCAIS	AMERICAN ENGLISH	ITALIANO	DEUTSCH	ESPAÑOL
689	Incise	Rhythmic group	Inciso	Incisum	Inciso
690	Système	System	Sistema	System	Sistema
691	Chironomie	Chironomy	Chironomía	Cheironomie	Quironomía
692	Allitération	Alliteration	Accidente	Stabreim	Aliteracíon
693	Scander	To scan	Scandire	Hervorheben	Medir
694	Scansion	Metrical scansion	Metrica	Skandiren	Metrica
695	HARMONIE	HARMONY	ARMONIA	HARMONIELEHRE	ARMONIA
696	Harmonisation	Harmonisation	Armonizzazione	Harmonisierung	Armonización
697	Accord	Chord	Accordo	Akkord	Acorde
698	L'accord	The state of being in tune	Accordo	Akkord Stimmen	Acorde
699	Tonalité	Tonality Key	Tonalita	Tonart Tonalität	Tonalidad
700	Gamme	Scale	Scala	Tonleiter Skala	Escala
701	Armure	Key signature	Armatura (di chiave)	Vorzeichnung (Schlüsselvorzeichnung	Armadura de clave
702	Enharmonie	Enharmonic	Enarmonía	Enharmonie	Enarmonía
703	Ton relatif	Relative key Relative tonality	Tono relativo	Paralleltonart	Tono relativo
704	Accord altéré	Altered chord	Accordo alterato	Alteriert	Acorde alterado
705	Accord de seconde	Two-chord (Chord in third inversion)	Accordo di seconda	Sekundeakkord	Acorde de segunda
706	Accord de sixte	Six-chord (chord in first inversion)	Accordo di sesta	Sextakkord	Acorde de sexta
707	Accord de quarte et sixte	Six-four chord (second inversion)	Accordo di quarta e sesta	Quartsextakkord	Acorde de cuarta y sexta Acorde en segunda inversión
708	Accord de septième diminuée	Diminished-seventh chord	Accordo di settima diminuita	Verminderter Septakkord	Acorde de séptima disminuída
709	Accord neutre	Neutral chord	Accordo neutro	Neutraler akkord	Acorde neutro
710	Hexacorde	Hexachord	Esaccordo	Hexachord	Hexacorde
711	Conduite des voix	Voice-leading	Movimento di voci	Stimmführung	Conducción de las voces

N°	FRANCAIS	AMERICAN ENGLISH	ITALIANO	DEUTSCH	ESPAÑOL
712	Voix inter-médiaires	Inner voices	Voci intermediarie	Mittel stimmen	Voces intermedias Voces intermediarias Voces internas
713	Bourdon	Bourdon	Bordone	Schnarrbass Hummelbass	Bordón
714	Faux-bourdon	Fauxbourdon	Falso bordone	Freie choral begleitung	Falso bordón
715	Fausse relation	False relation Cross relation	Falsa relazione	Querstand	Falsa relación
716	Anticipation	Anticipation	Anticipazione	Vorausnahme	Anticipación
717	Préparation	Preparation	Preparazione	Vorbereitung	Preparación
718	Résolution	Resolution	Risoluzione	Auflösung	Resolución
719	Retard	Suspension	Ritardo	Vorhalt	Retardo
720	Position	Position	Posizione	Lage	Posición
720b	Demi-position	Half-position	Semiposizione	Mittellage	Semiposición
721	Broderie	Nonharmonic tone	Bordatura	Broderie	Bordadura
722	Appogiature	Appoggiatura	Appoggiatura	Appogiatura Unvorbereiteter Vorhalt	Apogiatura Apoyatura
723	Marche harmonique	Harmonic movement	Movimento armonico	Harmonische Fortschreitung	Marcha armónica
724	Enchaînement	Linking	Incatenamento	Verbindung	Encadenamiento
725	Progression ascendante	Ascending progression	Progressione ascendente	Steigende Fortschreitung	Progresión ascendente
726	Progression descendante	Descending progression	Progressione discendente	Fallende fortschreitung	Progresión descendente
727	Croisement	Crossing(of voices)	Incrosciamento	Kreuzung	Cruzamiento
728	Rapport avec la sous-dominante mineure	Relation of the sub-dominant minor	Rapporto colla sottodominante minore	Beziehung zur Moll-Unterdomi-nante	Relación con la subdomi-nãnte menor
729	Octaves et quin-tes parallèles	Parallel octaves Parallel fifths	Ottave e quinte parallele	Oktaven und Quinten Parallelen	Octavas y quintas paralelas
730	Cycle de quintes ascendantes	Cycle of fifths, ascending	Ciclo di quinte ascendenti	Quintenzirkel aufwärts	Círculo de quintas ascendentes
731	Cycle de quintes descendantes	Cycle of fifths, descending	Ciclo di quinte descendenti	Quintenzirkel abwärts	Círculo de quintas descendentes
732	Quintes cachées	Hidden fifths	Quinte nascoste	Verdeckte quinten	Quintas superpuestas
733	Sixte napolitaine	Neapolitan sixth	Sesta napoletana	Neapolitanische Sext	Sexta napolitana

N°	FRANCAIS	AMERICAN ENGLISH	ITALIANO	DEUTSCH	ESPAÑOL
734	Dominantes secondaires	Secondary dominants	Dominante secondarie	Nebendominanten	Dominantes secundarias
735	Consonance	Consonance	Consonanza	Konsonanz	Consonancia
736	Dissonance	Dissonance	Dissonanza	Dissonanz	Disonancia
737	Cadence	Cadence	Cadenza	Kadenz	Cadencia
738	Cadentiel	Cadential	Cadenzato	Kadenz artig	Cadencial
739	Cadence parfaite	Perfect cadence	Cadenza perfetta	Vollkommene kadenz	Cadencia perfecta
740	Cadence impar-faite	Imperfect cadence	Cadenza imperfetta	Unvollkommene kadenz	Cadencia imperfecta
741	Cadence plagale	Plagal cadence	Cadenza sospesa	Plagalschluss	Cadencia plagal
742	Cadence rompue	Interrupted cadence	Cadenza rotta	Trugschluss	Cadencia rota
743	Modulation	Modulation	Modulazione	Modulation	Modulación
744	Séquence	Sequence	Sequenza	Sequenz	Secuencia
745	Fonctions tonales	Tonal functions	Funzioni tonali	Tonale funktionen	Funciones tonales
746	Fondamentale	Fundamental	Fondamentale	Grundton Fundament	Fundamental
747	Pas ascendant	Ascending steps Ascending leaps	Passo ascendente	Steigender Fundamentschritt	Salto ascendente
748	Pas de seconde	Step of a second	Passo di seconda	Sekundenschritt	Salto de segunda
749	Pas de tierce	Leap of a third	Passo di terza	Terzenschritt	Salto de tercera
750	Pas de quarte	Leap of a fourth	Passo di quarta	Quartenschritt	Salto de cuarta
751	Pas de quinte	Leap of a fifth	Passo di quinte	Quintenschritt	Salto de quinta
752	Basse chiffrée	Figured bass	Basso cifrato	Generalbass Bezifferung	Bajo cifrado
753	Basse donnée	Given bass	Basso dato	Generalbass	Bajo dado
754	Basse continue	Continuous bass	Basso continuo	Continuo	Bajo continuo
755	Chiffrage	The figuring of... Figures	Cifrato	Bezifferung	Cifrado
756	Basse contrainte	Ground bass	Basso continuo	Obligater Bass	Bajo obligado
757	Pédale	Pedal	Pedale	Pedal	Pedal
758	Note ajoutée	Added note	Nota aggiunta	Beigefügte note	Nota agregada
759	Note étrangère	Foreign note	Nota strana	Harmonie fremde note	Nota ajena
760	CONTREPOINT	COUNTER-POINT	CONTRAPPUNTO	KONTRAPUNKT	CONTRAPUNTO
761	Libre	Free	Libero	Frei	Libre

N°	FRANCAIS	AMERICAN ENGLISH	ITALIANO	DEUTSCH	ESPAÑOL
762	Rigoureux	Rigorous Strict	Rigoroso	Streng	Riguroso
763	Contrepoint simple	Simple counterpoint	Contrappunto semplice	Einfacher Kontrapunkt	Contrapunto simple
764	Contrepoint composé	Composed counterpoint	Contrappunto composto	Zusammengesetzter Kontrapunkt	Contrapunto compuesto
765	Contrepoint double	Double counterpoint	Contrappunto doppio	Doppelter Kontrapunkt	Contrapunto doble
766	Contrepoint triple	Triple counterpoint	Contrappunto triplo	Dreifacher Kontrapunkt	Contrapunto triple
767	Contrepoint quadruple	Quadruple counterpoint	Contrappunto quadruplo	Vierfacher Kontrapunkt	Contrapunto cuádruple
768	Contrepoint libre	Free counterpoint	Contrappunto libero	Freier Kontrapunkt	Contrapunto libre
769	Contrepoint de première espèce	Counterpoint in first species	Contrappunto prima specie	Kontrapunkt der ersten gattung	Contrapunto de primera especie
770	A plusieurs voix	In several voices	a varie voci	Mehrstimming	A varias voces
771	Contrepoint fleuri	Florid counterpoint	Contrappunto fiorito	Ausgeschmückter Kontrapunkt	Contrapunto florido
772	Contrepoint renversable	Invertible counterpoint	Contrappunto rovesciabile	Umkehrbarer Kontrapunkt	Contrapunto reversible
773	Contrepoint avec syncopes	Syncopated counterpoint	Contrappunto sincopato	Kontrapunkt mit syn-kopierter gegenstimme	Contrapunto sincopado
774	Mélange	Mixture	Mescolanza	Mixtur	Mezcla
775	Grand mélange	Total mixture	Grande mesco-lanza	Gesammtkontra-punkt	Contrapunto total Gran mezcla
776	Sujet	Subject	Soggetto	Subjekt	Sujeto
777	Contre-sujet	Counter-subject	Contrasoggetto	Kontrasubjekt Gegenthema	Contrasujeto
778	Contre-chant	Contrasubject	Contrasoggetto	Gegensatz	Contrasujeto Contracanto
779	Augmentation	Augmentation	Aumento	Vergrösserung	Aumentación
780	Amplification	Amplification	Amplificazione	Verstärkung Erweiterung	Amplificación
781	Diminution	Diminution	Diminuzione	Verkleinerung	Disminución Diminución
782	Imitation	Imitation	Imitazione	Nachahmung	Imitación
783	Réplique	Replica	Repplica	Wiederholung des themas	Réplica

N°	FRANCAIS	AMERICAN ENGLISH	ITALIANO	DEUTSCH	ESPAÑOL
784	**FUGUE**	FUGUE	**FUGA**	FUGE	FUGA
785	**Fugué**	Fugue-like	**Fugato**	Fugiert	Fugado
786	**Double-fugue**	Double-fugue	**Doppia fuga**	Doppelfuge	Doble fuga
787	**Triple fugue**	Triple-fugue	**Triplo fuga**	Tripelfuge	Triple fuga
788	**à plusieurs voix**	In several voices	**A varie voci**	Mehrstimmig	A varias voces
789	**Sujet**	Subject	**Soggetto** Tema	Thema Haupsatz Fugenthema	Sujeto
790	**Contre-sujet**	Counter-subject	**Contrassoggetto**	Gegensatz Gegenthema	Contrasujeto
791	**Exposition**	Exposition	**Esposizione**	Exposition	Exposición
792	**Contre-exposition**	Counter exposition	**Contraesposizione**	Gegenexposition	Contraexposición
793	**Réexposition**	Re-exposition	**Riesposizione**	Reprise	Reexposición
794	**Préparation**	Preparation	**Preparazione**	Vorbereitung	Preparación
795	**Culmination**	Culmination	**Culminazione**	Höhenlage	Culminación
796	**Réponse**	Response	**Risposta**	Beantwortung	Respuesta
797	**Développement**	Development	**Sviluppo**	Durchführung	Desarrollo
798	**Divertissement**	Divertimento	**Divertimento**	Divertissement	Divertimento
799	**Antécédent**	Antecedent	**Antecedente**	Dux Führer (in der fuge)	Antecedente
800	**Conséquent**	Consequent	**Consequente**	Nachfolgende stimme	Consecuente
801	**Désinence**	Conclusion Ending	**Desinenza**	Endung Desinenz	Desinencia
802	**Réplique**	Repeat	**Repplica**	Wiederholung eines thema	Réplica
803	**Mutation**	Mutation, Variation Alteration	**Mutazione**	Mutation Hexachordwechsel	Mutación
804	**Strette**	Stretto	**Stretto**	Stretta Engführung	Estrecho Stretto
805	**Coda**	Coda	**Coda**	Koda	Coda
806	**Mouvement parallèle**	Parallel motion	**Movimiento parallelo**	Parallele bewegung	Movimiento paralelo
807	**Mouvement contraire**	Contrary motion	**Movimento contrario**	Gegenbewegung	Movimiento contrario
808	**Phrase musicale**	Musical phrase	**Frase musicale**	Satz - Phrase	Frase

N°	FRANCAIS	AMERICAN ENGLISH	ITALIANO	DEUTSCH	ESPAÑOL
809	FORME MUSICALE	MUSICAL FORM	FORMA MUSICALE	FORMEN	FORMA MUSICAL
810	Forme cyclique	Cyclic form Cyclical form	Forma ciclic	Zyklische sonatenform	Forma cíclica
811	Thème	Theme	Tema	Thema	Tema
812	Thématisme	Thematicism	Tematismo	Thematik	Tematismo
813	Thématique	Thematic	Tematico	Thematik	Temático
814	Bi-thématisme Di-thématisme	Bi-thematic	Bitematico	Doppel Zweifacher thematik Mehfacher Tematik	Bitematismo Ditematismo
815	Thème varié	Varied theme	Tema con variazioni	Variertes thema	Tema variado Tema con variaciones
816	Variation	Variation	Variazione	Variation	Variación
817	Variation continue	Continuous variation	Variazione continua	Fortlaufende variation	Variación continua
818	Variation ornementale	Ornamental variation	Variazione ornementale	Ornamentierte variation	Variación ornemental
819	Variation amplificatrice	Durational variation	Variazione per amplificazione	Entwickelnde variation	Variación por amplificación
820	Conduit	Bridge Transition	Passaggio Ponte	Kleine überleitung	Pasaje Punto
821	Sonate	Sonata	Sonata	Sonate	Sonata
822	Forme lied	Song-form	Forma lied	Liedartig	Forma lied
823	Divertissement	Divertimento	Divertimento	Divertissement	Divertimento
824	Rondeau	Rondeau Rondo	Rondo	Rondo	Rondo Rondeau
825	Suite	Suite	Suite	Suite	Suite
826	Partita	Partita	Partita	Partita	Partita
827	Prélude	Prelude	Preludio	Vorspiel Präludium	Preludio
828	Ouverture	Overture	Ovverture	Ouvertüre	Obertura
829	Ouverture à la française	French overture	Ovverture alla franchese	Französische Ouvertüre	Obertura francesa
830	Ouverture à l'italienne	Italian overture	Ovverture alla italiana	Italianische Ouvertüre Sinfonia	Obertura italiana
831	Allemande	Allemande	Alemanna	Allemande	Allemande Alemana

N°	FRANCAIS	AMERICAN ENGLISH	ITALIANO	DEUTSCH	ESPAÑOL
832	Courante	Courante	Corrente	Courante Corrente	Courante Corrente
833	Sarabande	Sarabande	Sarabanda	Sarabande	Sarabanda
834	Menuet	Minuet	Minuetto	Menuett	Minué
835	Gavotte	Gavotte	Gavotta	Gavotte	Gavota
836	Musette	Musette	Musetta	Musette	Musette
837	Double	Double	Double (Variazione)	Doppelt Dublette	Double Variación
838	Bourrée	Bourree	Bourrée	Bourrée	Bourrée
839	Gaillarde	Galliard	Gagliarda	Gaillarde	Gallarda
840	Sicilienne	Siciliana	Siciliana	Sizilischer tanz	Siciliana
841	Chaconne	Chaconne	Ciaccona	Chaconne	Chacona
842	Passacaille	Passacaglia	Passacaglia	Passacaille Passacaglia	Pasacalle
843	Cavatine	Cavatina	Cavatina	Cavatine	Cavatina
844	Rondo	Rondo	Rondo	Rondo	Rondo
845	Gigue	Gigue	Giga	Gigue Hopfer	Giga Jiga
846	Concerto	Concerto	Concerto	Konzert	Concierto
847	Symphonie	Symphony	Sinfonia	Symphonie	Sinfonía
848	Symphonie de chambre	Chamber symphony	Sinfonia da camera	Kammersymphonie	Sinfonía de cámara
849	Poème symphonique	Symphonic poem	Poema sinfonico	Tondichtung	Poema sinfónico
850	Introduction	Introduction	Introduzzione	Einführung Einleitung	Introducción
851	Strophe	Strophe	Strofa	Strophe	Estrofa
852	Ritournelle	Ritornello	Ritornello	Ritornell	Ritornello
853	Refrain	Refrain	Ritornello Canzone	Wiederholungs Strophe	Estribillo
854	Couplet	Couplet	Strofa	Strophe	Estrofa
855	Final	Finale	Finale	Final Schlussteil	Final
856	Canon	Canon	Canone	Canon	Canon
857	Choral	Choral	Corale	Choral	Coral
858	Choral varié	Chorale variation	Corale con varianti	Variertes choral	Coral variado

N°	FRANCAIS	AMERICAN ENGLISH	ITALIANO	DEUTSCH	ESPAÑOL
859	Choral figuré	Figured choral tune	Corale florido	Figuriertes choral	Coral figurado Coral florido
860	Cantate	Cantata	Cantata	Kantate	Cantata
861	Motet	Motet	Mottetto	Motette	Motete
862	Messe	Mass	Messa	Messe	Misa
863	Réquiem	Requiem	Requiem	Seelenmesse Requiem Trauermesse	Requiem Misa de difuntos
864	Oratorio	Oratorio	Oratorio	Oratorium	Oratorio
865	Passion	Passion	Passione	Passion	Pasión
866	Psaume	Psalm	Salmodia	Psalm	Salmo
867	Récitatif	Recitatif Recitativo	Recitativo	Rezitativ	Recitativo
868	Madrigal	Madrigal	Madrigale	Madrigal	Madrigal
869	Anthem	Anthem	Inno Antifona	Anthem	Antifona
870	Antienne	Antiphon Anthem	Antifona	Vorgesang	Antifona
871	Hymne	Hymn Anthem	Inno	Hymne	Himno
872	Chanson	Song Chanson	Canzone	Liedchen	Canción
873	Ballade	Ballad Ballade	Ballata	Ballade	Balada
874	Berceuse	Lullaby	Ninnananna	Wiegenlied	Canción de cuna
875	Aubade	Morning music	Albata	Morgenständchen	Alborada
876	Barcarolle	Barcarole	Barcarola	Barcarole	Barcarola
877	Cassation	Cassation	Cassazione	Kassation	Casación
878	Etude	Study Etude	Studio	Studie Etüde	Estudio
879	Fantaisie	Fantasy	Fantasia	Fantasie	Fantasia
880	Interlude	Interlude	Interludio Intermezzo	Zwischenspiel	Interludio
881	Intermède	Intermezzo	Intermezzo	Intermezzo Mukalisches Zwis-chenspiel	Intermedio
882	Impromptu	Impromptu	Impromptu	Impromptu	Impromptu
883	Invention	Invention	Invenzione	Invention	Invención

N°	FRANCAIS	AMERICAN ENGLISH	ITALIANO	DEUTSCH	ESPAÑOL
884	Nocturne	Nocturne	Notturni	Nokturno	Nocturno
885	Quatuor	Quartet	Quartetto	Quartett	Cuarteto
886	Romance	Romance	Romanza	Romanze	Romance
887	Rhapsodie	Rhapsody	Rapsodia	Rhapsodie	Rapsodia
888	Scherzo	Scherzo	Scherzo	Scherzo	Scherzo
889	Sérénade	Serenade	Serenata	Serenade	Serenata
890	Air de cour	Court air	Aria di corte	Hofarie	Aire de corte
891	Ballet	Ballet	Balletto	Ballet	Ballet
892	Contredance	Contredanse	Contradanza	Contratanz Englischer reihen	Contradanza
893	Laude	Laude	Laude	Lobgesänge	Laude
894	Sautereau	Saltarello	Saltarello	Docke	Saltarello
895	Valse	Waltz	Valzer	Walzer	Vals
896	Villanelle	Villanella	Villanella	Canzonetta	Villanela
897	Virelai	Virelai	Virelai Ritornello	Ringellied	"Virelai" Ringellied
898	Marche	March	Marcia	Marsch	Marcha
899	Pot-pourri	Potpourri	Pot-pourri	Potpourri	Popurrí
900	COMPOSITION	COMPOSITION	COMPOSIZIONE	KOMPOSITION	COMPOSICIÓN
901	Compositeur	Composer	Compositore	Komponist	Compositor
902	Improvisation	Improvisation	Improvvisazione	Improvisation	Improvisación
903	Improvisateur	Improviser	Improvvisatore	Improvisator	Improvisador
904	Noter	Notate	Notare	In noten setzen	Escribir
905	Motif	Motif Motive	Motivo	Motive	Motivo
906	Paramètre	Parameter	Parametro	Parameter	Parámetro
907	Notation proportionnelle	Proportional notation	Notazione proporzionale	Mensuralnotation	Escritura proporcional
908	Notation carrée	Square notation	Notazione quadrata	Quadratnotation	Notacion cuadrada Escritura cuadrada
909	Renversement	Inversion	Rivoltato	Umkehrung	Inversión
910	Récurrence	Recurrence	Ricusa Ostinato	Krebs	Recurrencia
911	Renversement récurrent	Recurrent inversion	Rovesciamento ricorrente	Krebsumkehrung	Inversión recurrente
912	Prosodie	Versification Metrical structure	Prosodia	Prosodie Betonung	Prosodia

N°	FRANCAIS	AMERICAN ENGLISH	ITALIANO	DEUTSCH	ESPAÑOL
913	Procédé de liquidation	Liquidation technique	Procedimento di liquidazione	Liquidierungs Prozess	Proceso de liquidación
914	Agogique	Agogic	Agogica	Agogik	Agógica
915	Au mouvement	A tempo At original tempo	A tempo	Im Zeitmass	A tempo
916	Non mesuré	Not measured	Senza mesura	Mit aufgehobenem Zeitmass	Sin medir
917	Sans rigueur	Freely Without rigor	Senza rigore Libero	Ohne Strenge Locker	Libero Sin medida
918	En accélérant	Quickening Accelerando	Accelerando	Beschleunigend	Acelerando
919	En ralentissant	Slowing down Rallentando	Rallentando	Langsamer werden	Ralentando
920	En retardant	Slowing down	Ritardando	Etwas zögernd	Retardando
921	En retenant	Holding back	Ritenuto	Zurückhaltend	Ritenuto
922	En élargissant	Broadening	Allargando	Breiter werdend	Alargando
923	Sans presser	Without hurrying	Senza affretare	Nicht beschleunigen	Sin apresurar
924	Sans lenteur	Without slowness	Senza rallentare	Nicht schleppen	Sin ralentar
925	Allant	Moving	Andante	Fliessend	Moviendo
926	Soutenu	Sustained	Sostenuto	Gehalten	Sostenido
927	Serré	Tighten	Prestissimo	Eng	Lo mas rápido posible Prestísimo
928	Caractère	Character	Carattere	Charakter	Carácter
929	Grave	Grave	Grave	Ernsthaft Düster	Grave
930	Large	Broad	Largo	Breit	Largo
931	Lent	Slow	Lento	Langsam	Lento
932	Pesant	Heavy	Pesante	Gewichtig Schwer	Pesante
933	Modéré	Moderate	Moderato	Mässig bewegt	Moderado
934	Animé	Animated	Animato	Belebt	Animado
935	Léger	Light	Leggiero	Leicht	Ligero
936	Vif	Lively	Vivace	Rasch	Vivo
937	Très vif	Very lively	Molto vivace	Sehr rasch	Muy vivo
938	Plus vite	More lively	Più presto	Schneller	Más vivo

N°	FRANCAIS	AMERICAN ENGLISH	ITALIANO	DEUTSCH	ESPAÑOL
939	Filer (un son)	To sustain	Scemar di voce	Einen Ton lange Aushalten Spinnen	Filar Hilar
940	Lié	Slurred Legato	Legato	Gebunden	Legato
941	Coulé	Slur	Legato	Geschleift Schleifer	Ligado
942	Détaché	Detached	Staccato	Abtragen	Destacado
943	Vibrer	Vibrate	Vibrare	Schwingen	Vibrar
944	Attaque	Attack	Attacco	Anschlag	Ataque
945	Entrée	Entrance	Attacco	Einsatz	Entrada Ataque
946	Louré	Louré Portato	Portato	Geschleift	Arrastrado
947	Piqué	Stung Sharply	Pizzicato	Gestossen Pikiert	Picado Pizzicato
948	Etouffer	Dampen	Smorzare	Dämpfen	Apagar
949	Divisé	Divided	Separato	Geteilt	Dividido
950	Expression	Expression	Espressione	Ausdrück	Expresión
951	Accentuation	Accentuation	Accentazione Attacco	Betonung Akzent	Acentuación
952	Nuance	Dynamics	Colore "Nuance"	Nuance	Dinámica
953	En dehors	Outstanding	In rilievo	Hervor Hervortreten	En relieve
954	Précis	Precise	Preciso	Bestimmt Präzis	Preciso Exacto
955	Arpège	Arpeggio	Arpeggio	Arpeggio	Arpegio
956	Arpégé	Arpeggiated	Arpeggiato	Arpeggiert	Arpegiado
957	Accord brisé	Broken chord	Accordo arpeggiato	Gebrochener Akkort	Acorde arpegiado
958	Respiration	Breathing pause	Respiro	Luftpause	Respiración
959	Césure	Pause Cesura Cut	Cesura	Zäsur	Cesura
960	Virgule	Comma	Virgola	Komma	Coma Cesura Respiración
961	Phrasé	Phrased	Fraseggio	Phrasierung	Fraseo

N°	FRANCAIS	AMERICAN ENGLISH	ITALIANO	DEUTSCH	ESPAÑOL
962	Liaison	Slur Legato Mark	Legatura	Bindung	Ligadura
963	Reprise	Reprise Repetition	Ripetizione	Reprise	Repetición
964	Renvoi	Repeat (al segno)	Segno	Wiederholungszeichen	Al segno
965	Ambitus	Ambitus Range	Ambito	Bereïch Umfang	Ambito
966	Episode	Episode	Episodio	Episode Zwischen Handlung Nebenmotiv	Episodio
967	Incise	Cesura Cut	Inciso	Einschnitt	Inciso
968	Roulade	Roulade	Gorgheggio	Läufer	Trino
969	MUSICOLOGIE	MUSICOLOGY	MUSICOLOGIA	MUSIKWISSENS-CHAFT	MUSICOLOGÍA
970	Musicologue	Musicologist	Musicologo	Musikschrifsteller	Musicólogo
971	Transcription	Transcription	Trascrizione	Bearbeitung	Transcripción
972	Analyse	Analyze	Analisi	Formenlehre	Análisis
973	EDITION MUSICALE	MUSICAL PUBLICATION	EDIZIONE MUSICALE	MUSIKVERLAG	EDICIÓN MUSICAL
974	Partition	Score	Partitura	Partitur	Partitura
975	Partition d'orchestre	Orchestral score	Partitura di orchestra	Orchesterpartitur	Partitura de orquesta
976	Partition de poche	Pocket score	Partitura di tasca	Taschenpartitur	Partitura de bolsillo
977	Partie d'orchestre	Orchestral part	Parte de orchestra	Orchester partie	Parte de orquesta
978	Matériel d'orchestre	Set of parts Material	Materiale di orchestra	Orchester material	Material de orquesta
979	Guidon	Guide score	Partitura guida	Kustos	Partitura de guía
980	Conducteur	Condensed score	Conduttore	Erleichterte klavier-auszug	Conductor
981	Réduction	Reduction	Riduzione	Reduzierung	Reducción
982	Première fois	First time	Prima volta	Das erste mal	Primera vez
983	Deuxième fois	Second time	Seconda volta	Das zweite mal	Segunda vez
984	Pochette	Pocket fiddle	Violino Piccolo	Taschengeige	Violín pequeño
985	Calques	Onion-skin transparencies	Lucidi	Durchzeichnung	Vegetales Calcos

N°	FRANCAIS	AMERICAN ENGLISH	ITALIANO	DEUTSCH	ESPAÑOL
986	Epreuve	Proof	Prova	Korrekturbogen	Corrección Prueba
987	Correcteur	Proofreader Corrector	Correttore	Korrektur	Corrector
988	Révision	Revision	Revisione	Revidirung	Revisión
989	Droits d'auteur	Authors'rights	Diritto d'autore	Rechte	Derechos de autor
990	Copie musicale	Music copying	Copia musicale	Musikabschreiben	Copia musical
991	Copiste	Music copyist	Copista	Kopist Musikabschreiber	Copista
992	Gravure musicale	Musical engraving	Incizione	Notenstich	Grabación musical
993	Graveur	Engraver	Incisore	Notenstecher	Grabador de musica
994	Rastral	Claw Staff writer	Rastral	Rastral	Pluma pentagramada Rastral
995	Accordoir	Tuning hammer	Accordatore	Klavier-stimmschlü-ssel	Afinador
996	Clef d'accordeur	Tuner's key Tuner's hammer	Chiave d'accordare	Stimmschlüssel	Llave del afinador
997	Facture d'instruments	Instrument-making	Fabricazione di strumenti	Instrumentenbau	Fabricación de instrumentos
998	Facteur d'instruments	Instrument-maker	Fabbricante di strumenti	Instrumenten Macher	Fabricante de instrumentos
999	Luthier	Luthier	Liutaio	Saiteninstrumenten-macher	Violero Fabricante de instrumentos de cuerda Luthier
1000	Archetier	Bow-maker	Fabbricante di archi	Bogenmacher	Fabricante de arcos
1001	Critique musical	Music critic	Critica Musicale	Musikkritiker	Crítica musical